Kemet Scribe

HIEROGLYPHIC
SIGN LIST & VOCABULARY

EXTENDED EDITION

Authored By

Bernard Paul Badham

kemetscribe.com

ARK PUBLISHING

Ameni-amenna

Revised edition first published in Great Britain in 2019 by Ark Publishing.
Authors edition first self-published in 2015 by Bernard Paul Badham.
www.arkpublishing.co.uk

Extended Edition

ISBN-13: 978 1912418060

ISBN-10: 1912418060

Author

Bernard Paul Badham

Egyptologist, Author and Physicist. Born in Wales in 1950 Bernard has worked as a school and college lecturer and as the Head of Science at the British International School in Cairo from where he explored the ancient sites of Egypt for over a decade. Bernard is an author of many Egyptology publications and has created a series for students to learn how to read Ancient Egyptian hieroglyphics from foundation course to more advanced studies and exercises.

How to Read Hieroglyphics & Ancient Egyptian Art: *Examples & Exercises 1*

Unlock the mysteries of ancient Egypt. A comprehensive practical guide to reading the ancient scribal text of Egypt, packed with methods and 117 examples of translation, 8 vocabulary exercises and 8 translation exercises with answers.

ISBN: 978 1912418152

A Concise Chronicle of the Kings and Queens of Ancient Egypt

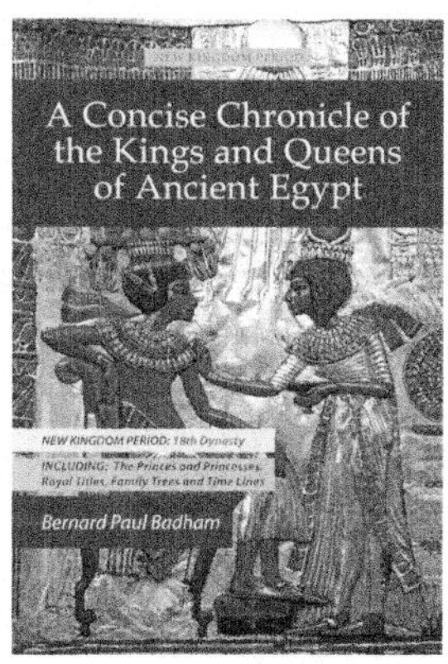

A Concise Chronicle of the Kings and Queens of Ancient Egypt including the Princes and Princesses, Royal Titles, Family Trees and Time Lines. Students of Egyptology and Hieroglyphics will find the book valuable as a quick reference guide to one of the most interesting dynasties of Ancient Egypt.

ISBN: 978 1912418107

CONTENTS

The Egyptian Phonetic Alphabet

Dictionary order and groups:

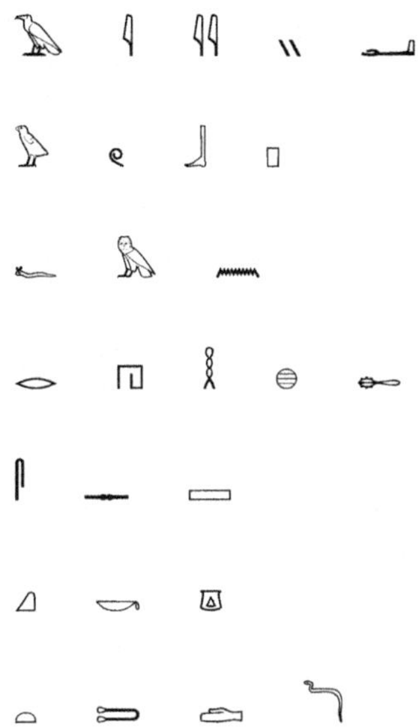

Sign	value	GN	description, phonetic sound
	A	G1	a vulture, sounds like 'a' as in 'father'
	i	M17	a flowering reed,sounds like 'i' as in 'bit'
	y	M17-M17	two flowering reed, sounds like 'y' as in 'try'
	y	Z4	two obleque strokes
	a	D36	forearm, sounds like 'a' as in 'cat'
	w	G43	quail chick
	w	Z7	spiral rope
	b	D58	foot

𓊪	**p**	**Q3**	stool
𓆑	**f**	**I9**	horned viper
𓅓	**m**	**G17**	owl
𓈖	**n**	**N35**	water
𓂋	**r**	**D21**	mouth
𓉔	**h**	**O4**	reed shelter, 'h' as in English
𓎛	**H**	**V28**	twisted flax, emphatic 'h'
𓐍	**x**	**Aa1**	sieve, 'ch' as in Scotish 'loch'
𓄡	**X**	**F32**	animal's belly, 'ch' as in German 'ich'
𓋴	**s**	**S29**	fold of cloth
𓊃	**z**	**O34**	door bolt
𓈙	**S**	**N37**	pool, 'sh' as in 'sheep'
𓈎	**q**	**N29**	hill side
𓎡	**k**	**V31**	basket with handle
𓎼	**g**	**W11**	jar stand
𓏏	**t**	**X1**	loaf of bread
𓍿	**T**	**V13**	a tethering rope
𓂧	**d**	**D46**	hand
𓆓	**D**	**I10**	snake, sounds like 'dj' in 'Djed'

SIGN LIST

SIGN LIST INDEX

KEY TO SIGN LIST

A quick reference key of tall narrow signs, low broad signs and low narrow signs. Use with the Sign List Index to find the page number.

TALL NARROW SIGNS

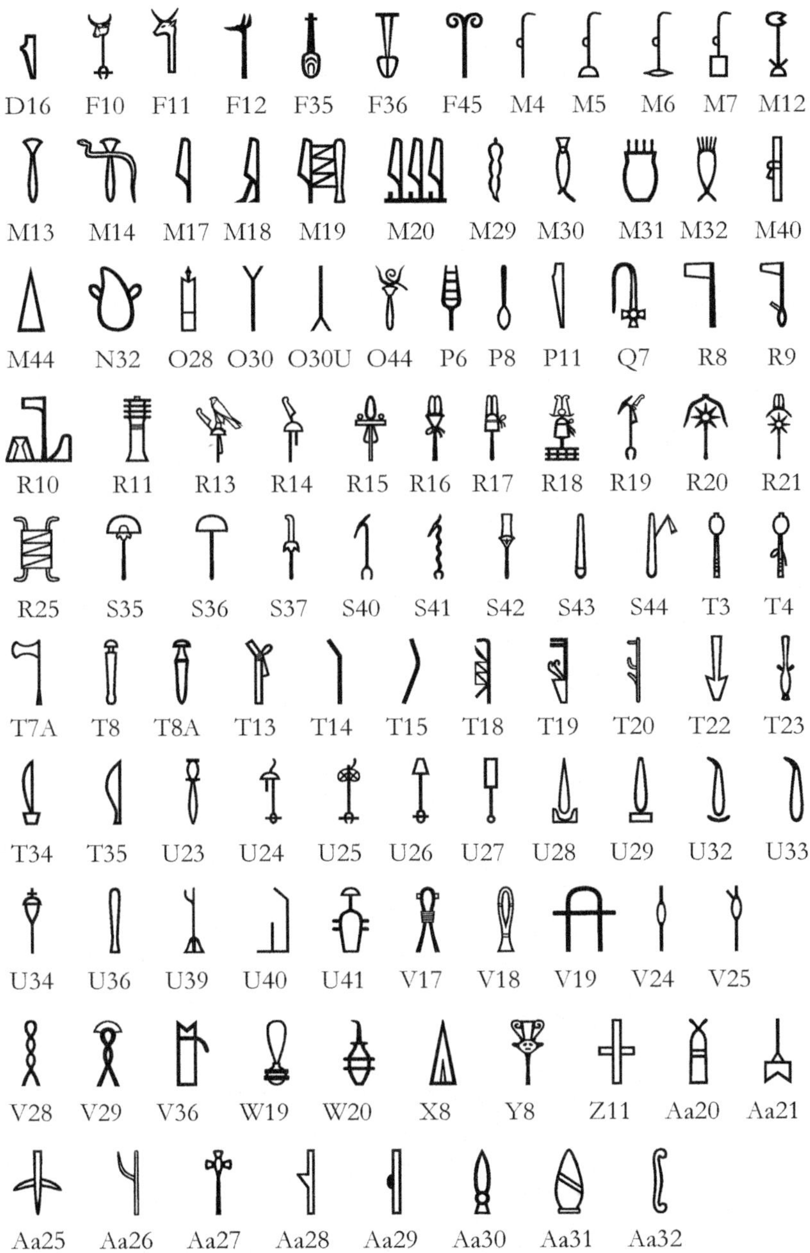

LOW BROAD SIGNS

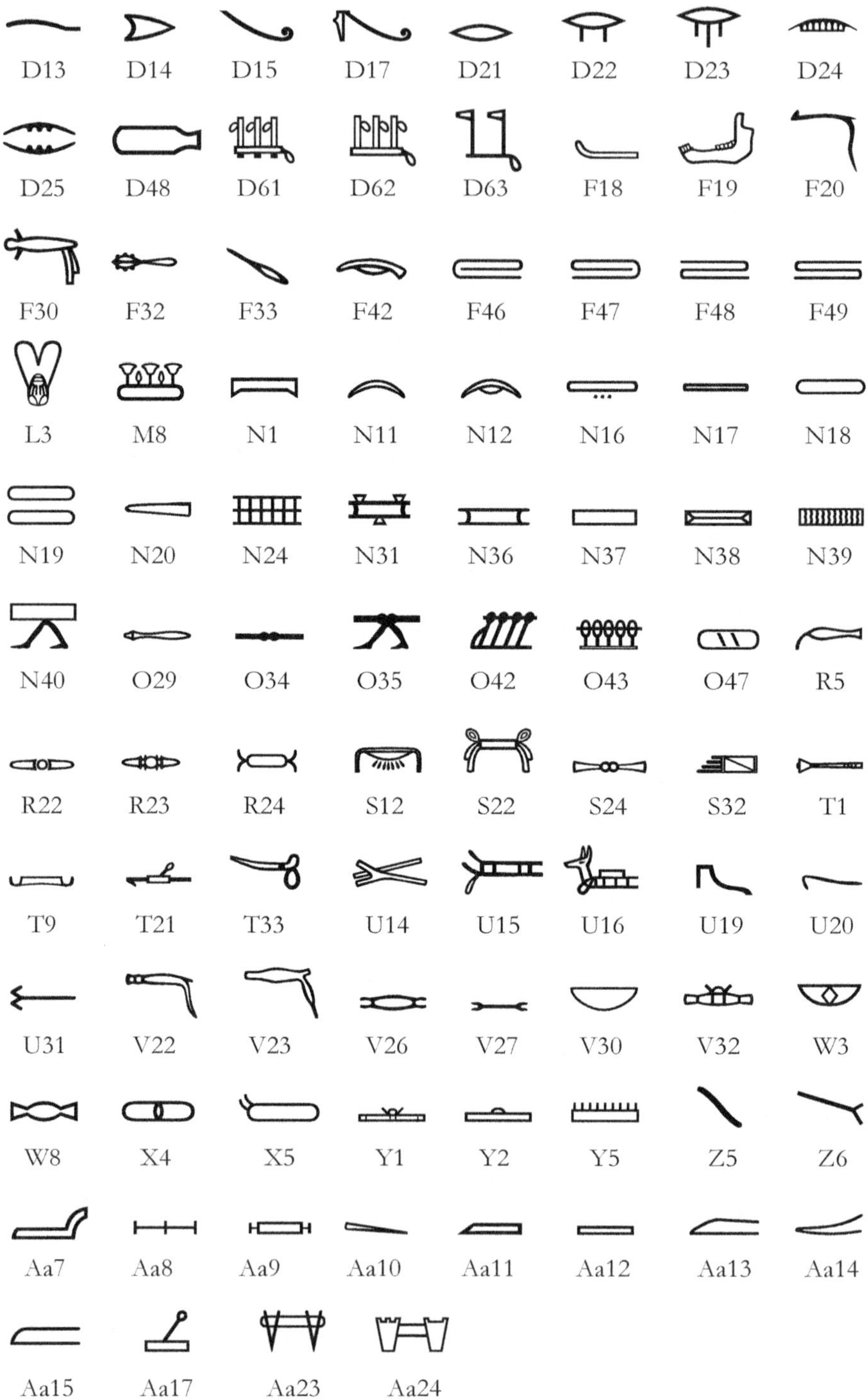

LOW NARROW SIGNS

SIGN LIST

A. Man and his occupations

A1-A55

A1		.i	seated man	**I, me, my, man**
A2			man with hand to mouth	**eat, hungry, drink, speak**
A3			man sitting on heel	**sit**
A4			man with arms raised	**adore**
A5			man hiding behind wall	**hide**
A6		**wab**	man receiving purification	**pure, clean**
A7			tired man	**weary, weak, faint**
A8			man performing rite	**jubilation**
A9		**kAt**	man with load on head	**load, carry, work**
A10			man with oar	**sail**
A11			man with sceptre and crook	**friend**
A12			soldier with bow and quiver	**army, soldiers**
A13			man, arms tied behind back	**enemy, rebel**
A14			man with axe to head	**die**

The Order: Gardiner's Code, Sign, Phonetic Sound, Description, Meaning.

A15		**xr**	man falling	**fall, fallen, overthrow**
A16			man bowing down	**bow down**
A17			child on lap	**child, orphan**
A18			child crown of Lower Egypt	**royal child, prince**
A19		**ik**	bent man on leaning on stick	**old, eldest, age, chief**
A20			bent man on forked stick	**eldest**
A21			man stick and handkerchief	**noble, official, courtier**
A22			statue with stick and sceptre	**statue**
A23			king with stick and mace	**sovereign**
A24			man striking stick two hands	**strike, force, plunder**
A25			man striking one hand	**strike**
A26			man one hand raised invocation	**call, summon, servant**
A27		**in**	man hastening two hands	**messenger**
A30			man two hands raised	**be high, rejoice, mourn**
A31			man with arms behind	**turn away, averted**
A32			man dancing	**dance, joy, jubilant**
A33			man with stick bundle	**herdsman, wander**
A34			man pounding mortar	**pound, build**
A35			man building wall	**build**
A36			man kneading in vessel	**brewer**
A37			man brewing	**brewer**
A38			man holding animal necks	**Cusae (a town)**
A39			man holding animal necks	**Cusae (a town)**

A40		seated god, curved beard	**god, I, me**
A41	**.i**	king with uraeus, curved beard	**king, majesty, I, me**
A42	**.i**	king, flagellum, curved beard	**king, majesty, I, me**
A43		king, white crown	**king, Osiris**
A44		king, flagellum, white crown	**king, Osiris**
A45		king, red crown	**king Lower Egypt**
A46		king, flagellum, red crown	**king Lower Egypt**
A47		seated sheperd	**herdsman, guard, protect**
A48		beardless man	**relating, belonging to**
A49		man holding stick	**foreigner, Asiatics**
A50	**.i/Sps**	nobleman on chair	**courtiers, I, me, noble**
A51		seated noble, flagellum	**noble, revered person**
A52	**Sps**	kneeling man, flagellum	**noble, revered person**
A53	**twt**	upright mummy	**mummy, statue, form**
A54		recumbent mummy	**death, sarcopagus**
A55		mummy on bed	**lie, spend night, death**

B. Woman and her Occupations

B1-B7

B1	**.i**	seated woman	**woman, wife, goddess**
B2		pregnant woman	**pregnant, conceive**
B3		woman giving birth	**bear, give birth**

B4		woman giving birth to **ms** sign	**bear, give birth**
B5		woman suckling child	**suckle, nurse, foster**
B6		seated woman with child	**nurse, rear**
B7		queen with diadem and flower	**names of queens**

C. Gods and Goddesses

C1-C12, C17-C20

C1		god with sun, uraeus	**Ra**
C2		god, falcon head	**Ra**
C3		god, ibis head	**Thoth** (**Djhwty**)
C4		god, ram head	**Khnum**
C5		god, ram head, ankh	**Khnum**
C6		god, jackal head	**Anubis, Wepwawet**
C7		god, seth head	**Seth**
C8		god, ithyphallic, feathers	**Min**
C9		goddess withh horns	**Hathor**
C10		goddess with Shu feather	**Maat**
C11	**HH**	god supporting sky	**Heh, million, many**
C12		god with **was** sceptre	**Amun**
C17		god holding ankh	**Mont**
C18		god kneeling, Atef crown	**Tjanen**

C19		god, **was** sceptre	**Ptah**
C20		god in booth	**Ptah**

D. Parts of Human Body

D1-D63

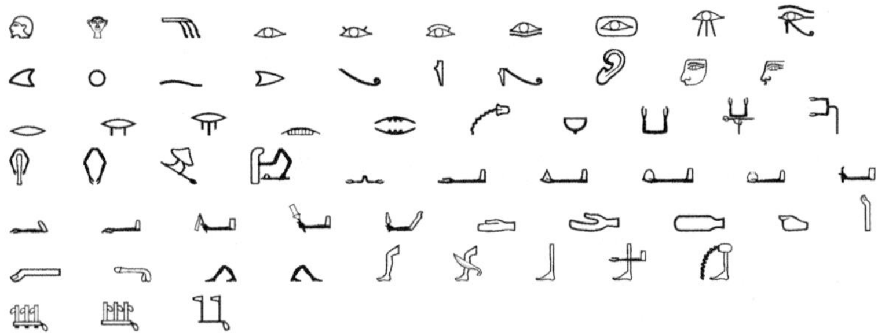

D1	**tp**	head in profile	**head, chief, first, on**
D2	**Hr**	face	**face, upon, because**
D3		hair	**hair, bald, skin**
D4	**irt**	eye	**eye, see, look, make**
D5		painted eye	**look, blind, be wakeful**
D6		eye, top eye lid	as D5
D7		eye, bottom eye lid	**adorn, paint eye**
D8		eye in land sign N18	**Ainu (Turah quarry)**
D9		eye, tears	**weep**
D10	**wDAt**	falcon eye	**left uninjured eye of Horus**
D11		right corner white part	**1/2 hekat of corn**

D12		pupil of eye	**1/4 hekat of corn**
D13		eyebrow	**1/8 hekat**
D14		left corner eye	**1/16 hekat**
D15		eye marking	**1/32 hekat**
D16		eye marking	**1/64 hekat**
D17		eye marking D15 and D16 image	
D18		ear	**ear**
D19	**fnd xnt**	nose, eye, cheek	**nose, smell, face, front**
D20		cursive D19	as D19
D21	**r**	mouth	**mouth, utterance**
D22	**rwy**	mouth 2 strokes	**2/3**
D23	**xmt-rw**	mouth 3 strokes	**3/4**
D24		upper lip, teeth	**lip, border**
D25	**spty**	two lips, teeth	**lips**
D26		liquid from mouth	**spit, vomit, blood**
D27		breast	**breast, suckle, tutor**
D28	**kA**	two arms	**ka, soul, spirit, work**
D29	**kA**	two arms on standard	**soul**
D30	**NHb-kAw**	two arms on bent standard	**serpent deity**
D31	**Hm-kA**	D32 and U36	**ka priest**
D32	**Hpt**	arms embracing	**envelop, embrace**
D33	**Xn**	arms rowing	**row, turmoil**
D34	**aHa**	arms holding shield, mace	**fight**
D35	**n**	arms in opposition	**negative, not, not know**

D36	**a**	forearm	**phonetic a, arm, hand**
D37	**di, mi**	offering bread X8	**to give**
D38	**mi, m**	offering loaf	**give, protect**
D39		offering pot	**present, offer**
D40	**nxt**	forearm holding stick	**strong, drag, examine**
D41	**ni**	bent arm palm down	**arm, shoulder, bend, bow**
D42	**mty**	palm down	**cubit measurement**
D43	**xw**	forearm, flagellum	**protect**
D44	**xrp**	forearm, sceptre	**control, administer**
D45	**Dsr**	forearm, **nHbt** wand	**holy, be private, clear**
D46	**d**	hand	**phonetic d, hand, put**
D47	**Drt**	curved hand	**hand**
D48	**Asp**	hand, no thumb	**palm, hand width**
D49	**ant**	fist	**grasp, seize**
D50	**Dba**	finger, vertical	**finger**
D51	**ant**	finger, horiz.	**nail**
D52	**mt, bA**	phallus	**poison, bull, capacity**
D53	**wsS**	phallus urinating	**male, urinate, poison**
D54	**iw**	legs walking towards	**come, go, approach**
D55	**ann**	legs walking away	**turn back, be reversed**
D56	**pds, war**	bent leg	**leg, foot, district, flee**
D57	**irT**	bent leg, knife T30	**mutilate, cheat**
D58	**b, bw**	leg and foot	phonetic **b, position**
D59	**ab**	leg, foot, hand D36	**horn**

D60		**wab**	leg, vase, water	**pure, clean, wab-priest**
D61		**saH**	toes	**toes, approach**
D62		**saH**	toes	as D61
D63		**saH**	toes	as D61

E. Mammals

E1-E34

E1		**kA**	bull	**bull, ox, cattle, herds**
E2		**kA nxt**	aggressive bull	**victorious/fighting bull**
E3		**bHs**	calf	**calf**
E4		**HsAt**	acred cow	**sacred cow**
E5		**Ams**	cow suckling calf	**show solicitude**
E6		**ssmt**	horse	**horse, stallion**
E7		**aA**	ass	**ass, donkey**
E8		**ib**	kid goat	**kid, thirst, refuge, flocks**
E9		**iw**	kid goat	**herds, refuge**
E10		**bA**	ram	**ram, sheep, Khnum**
E11		**bA**	ram (Old Kingdom)	**ram, sheep, Khnum**
E12			pig	**pig**
E13		**miw**	cat	**cat**

E14 		dog	**dog, hound**
E15 	**Inpw**	recumbent jackal	**Anubis**
E16 	**Inpw**	jackal on shrine	**Anubis**
E17 	**sAb**	jackal	**jackal, dignitary, worthy**
E18 		jackal on standard R12	**Wepwawet**
E19 		jackal on standard	**Wepwawet**
E20 	**stX**	Seth animal	**Seth, turmoil**
E21 		recumbent Set animal	**storm, rage**
E22 	**mAi**	lion	**lion**
E23 	**rw**	recumbent lion	**lion,** phonetic **r(w)**
E24 	**Aby**	panther	**panther, leopard**
E25 	**dib, xAb**	hippoptamus	**hippopotamus**
E26 	**Abw**	elephant	**elephant, Elephantine**
E27 	**sr**	giraffe	**foretell**
E28 	**mAHD**	oryx	**oryx**
E29 	**gHs**	gazelle	**gazelle**
E30 	**nAw**	ibex	**ibex**
E31 	**saH**	goat, cylinder seal	**rank, dignity**
E32 	**saH, ky**	sacred baboon	**baboon, monkey, furious**
E33 	**gf**	monkey	**monkey**
E34 	**wn**	desert hare	**exist, be, sale**

F. Parts of Mammals

F1-F52

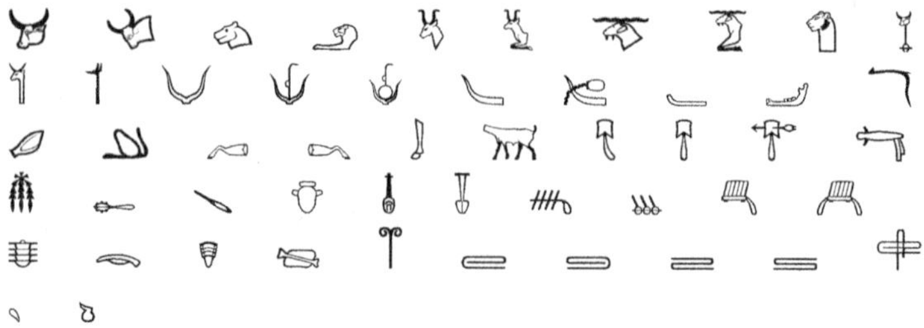

F1		**kA**	head of ox E1	in offering formula
F2		**D**	head of angry bull	**rage**
F3		**At**	head of hippopotamus	**striking power, attack**
F4		**HAt, HAty**	forepart of lion	**front, heart, prince**
F5		**SsAw, SsA**	head of bubalis E9	**bubalis, be skilled**
F6			forepart of bubalisas F5	
F7		**Sft, Sfyt**	ram's head	**worth, dignity**
F8			forepart of ram	as F7
F9		**pHty**	head of leopard	**strength**
F10		**xx, am**	long necked animal	**throat, swallow**
F11			long necked animal	as F10
F12		**wsrt, wsr**	head and neck of jackal	**neck, powerful, oar**
F13		**wpt**	horn of ox	**brow, beginning, open**
F14		**wpt-rnpt**	F13 and M4	**New Year's day**
F15			F13 and M4	as F14
F16		**ab**	horn	**horn, boast**
F17		**abw**	F16 and pot pouring water	**purification**

F18	**ibH, bH**	tusk of elephant	**tooth, calf**
F19	**art**	lower jawbone of ox	**jaw**
F20	**ns, imy-r**	tongue of ox	**tongue, he belongs to, overseer**
F21	**sDm, idn, msDr**	ear of ox	**hear, be deaf, ear**
F22	**pH**	hind-quarters of lion	**rear-end, end, reach**
F23	**xpS**	foreleg of ox	**foreleg, arm**
F24		F23 reversed	as F23
F25	**wHm**	leg of ox	**asses, repeat**
F26	**Xnt, Xnw**	body of goat	**skin, interior**
F27		cow's skin	**hide, skin, mamals**
F28		as F27	**variegated**
F29	**st**	cow's skin with arrow	**pierce**
F30	**Sd**	water skin	**water skin, cushion**
F31	**ms**	3 fox pelts tied	**give birth, apron**
F32	**Xt**	animal's belly	**belly, body**
F33	**sd**	tail	**tail**
F34	**ib**	heart	**heart**
F35	**nfr**	heart annd windpipe	**good, fine, beauty**
F36	**smA**	lung and windpipe	**lung, unite**
F37	**iAt**	back bon, ribs	**back**
F38	**psd**	as F37	**back**
F39	**imAx**	back bone, spinal chord	**venerated**
F40	**Awi**	back bone, spinal chord	**stretch out, offerings**
F41	**psd, sat**	vertebrae	**back, lust for blood**

F42	**spr**	rib	**rib, approach**
F43	**spHt**	ribs	**ribs of beef**
F44	**iwa, isw**	leg bone, beef	**tigh, inherit, exchange**
F45	**idt**	uterus of heifer	**vulva, cow**
F46	**qAb**	intestine	**intestine, double, turn**
F47		as F46	
F48		as F46	
F49		as F46	
F50	**spXr**	F46 and S29	**copy, write out**
F51	**As, ws**	piece of flesh	**limb, Isis, Osiris**
F52	**Hs**	excrement	**excrement**

G. Birds

G1-G54

G1	**A**	vulture	**vulture,** phonetic sound **A**
G2	**AA**	two vultures	**see**
G3	**mA**	G1 and U1	**renew**
G4	**tyw**	long legged buzzard	phonetic sound **tyw**

Sign	Transliteration	Description	Meaning
G5	**Hrw**	Horus falcon	**Horus**
G6	**bik**	falcon, flagellum	**falcon**
G7	**.I**	Horus standard	**Horus, gods, I, me**
G7A	**anty**	falcon on boat	**Anty (god)**
G7B	**anty**	falcon on boat	**Anty (god)**
G8	**Hrw-nbw**	golden Horus on S12	**Horus of Gold**
G9		Horus, sun disc	**Ra-Harakti**
G10	**skr**	falcon on sacred bark	**Sokar (god)**
G11		archaic falcon	**divine image, breast**
G12		G11 with flagellum	as G11
G13		G11 with plumes	**Horus of Nekhen**
G14	**nrt, mwt**	vulture	**vulture, mother**
G15	**mwt**	vulture with flagellum	**Mut** (mother goddess)
G16	**nbty**	vulture and cobra	**Two Ladies** (goddesses)
G17	**m**	owl	phonetic sound **m**
G18	**mm, im**	two owls	**not having been, therein**
G19	**m**	owl with D37	phonetic sound **m**
G20		owl with D36	as G19
G21	**nH**	guinea fowl	**nH-bird, pray, eternity**
G22	**Db**	hoopoe bird	**brick**
G23	**rHyt**	lapwing	**common folk**
G24		lapwing wings back	as G23
G25	**Ax**	crested ibis	**spirit, beneficial**
G26	**Hb**	ibis on standard	**ibis, Thoth (DHwty)**

G27		**Dsr**	flamingo	**flamingo, red**
G28		**gm, gmt, gmH**	black ibis	**find, ibis, look at**
G29		**bA**	jabiru stork	**soul, servant**
G30		**bAw**	three jabirus	**spirits, might**
G31		**bnw**	heron	**phoenix (benw bird)**
G32		**baHi**	heron on perch	**be inundated**
G33		**sdA**	egret	**sdA-bird, tremble**
G34		**niw**	ostrich	**ostrich**
G35		**aq**	cormorant	**enter, provisions**
G36		**wr**	swallow or martin	**great, anoint**
G37		**nDs**	sparrow	**small, bad, empty**
G38		**gb**	white fronted goose	**bird, goose, Geb** (god)
G39		**st, sA**	pintail duck	**duck, son**
G40		**pA**	pintail duck flying	**fly, the**
G41		**xnt, Tn**	pintail duck alighting	**alright, halt, distinguish**
G42		**wS**	fatted duck	**fatten, provisions**
G43		**w**	quail chick	phonetic sound **w**
G44		**ww**	two quail chicks	**end (phww)**
G45		**wa**	quail chick and D36	**soldier (waw)**
G46		**mAw**	quail chick with U1	**anew (m mAwt)**
G47		**TA**	duckling	**nestling**
G48		**sS**	three ducklings, nest	**nest**
G49		**sS**	three duck in pool	**bird-pool, nest**
G50		**rxty**	two plovers	**fuller, washerman**

G51		**HAm**	egret pecking fish	**catch fish**
G52		**snm**	goose pecking grain	**feed**
G53		**bA**	human-headed bird and R7	**soul (bA)**
G54		**wSn**	trussed bird	**wring neck, offer**

H. Parts of Birds

H1-H8

H1		**wSn**	head of duck	**fowl, wring neck, offer**
H2		**mAa, wSm**	head of crested bird	**temple, ear of corn**
H3		**pAq**	head of spoonbill	**cake**
H4		**nr**	head of vulture	**terror**
H5		**DnH, pA**	wing	**wing, fly**
H6		**Sw, mAat**	feather	**feather, truth, Shu (god)**
H6A		**Sw**	feather with two strokes	used in hieratic
H7		**SA**	claw	**Shat (the Land)**
H8		**st**	egg	**egg, son**

I. Amphibious Animals, Reptiles etc

I1-I15

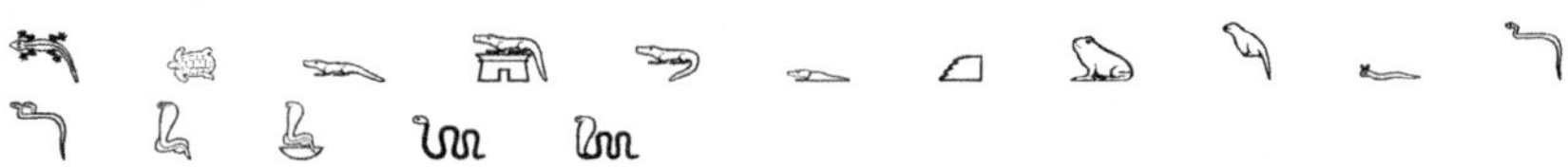

I1  **aSA** lizard **lizard, many**

I2  **Styw** freshwater turtle **turtle**

I3  **msH, it** crocodile **crocodile, sovereign**

I4  **sbk** crocodile on shrine **Sobek (crocodile god)**

I5  **sAq** crocodile curved tail **collect, gather together**

I5A **sbk** crocodile (archaic) **Sobek**

I6  **km** crocodile scales **Egypt (Kemet), shield**

I7  **Hqt** frog **Heket (frog goddess)**

I8  **Hfn** tadpole **100,000**

I9 **f** horned viper **father,** phonetic sound **f**

I10  **D** cobra **cobra,** phonetic sound **D** (dj)

I11  **DD** two cobras **what's been commanded**

I12  **iart** erect cobra **uraeus, goddess**

I13  cobra on basket V30 **Edjo (WADt, city of Buto), goddess**

I14  **HfAw** snake **serpent, worm**

I15  as I14

K. Fishes and Parts of Fish

K1-K7

K1  **in** fish **fish, valley, wall**

K2  **bw** fish **abomination**

K3		**ad**	fish	**administrator**
K4		**XA**	oxyrhynchus fish	**XAt-fish, corpse, widow**
K5		**bs**	fish	**introduce**
K6		**nSmt**	fish scale	**fish-scale**
K7		**Spt**	a fish	**be discontented**

L. Invertebrate and Lesser Animals

L1-L7

L1		**xpr**	dung beetle	**dung beetle, become**
L2		**bit**	bee of Lower Egypt	**bee, honey**
L3		**aff**	fly	**fly**
L4		**snHm**	locust	**locust**
L5		**spA**	centipede	**centipede**
L6		**xA**	bivalve shell	**offering table**
L7		**srqt**	scorpion	**Serket (goddess)**

M. Trees and Plants

M1-M44

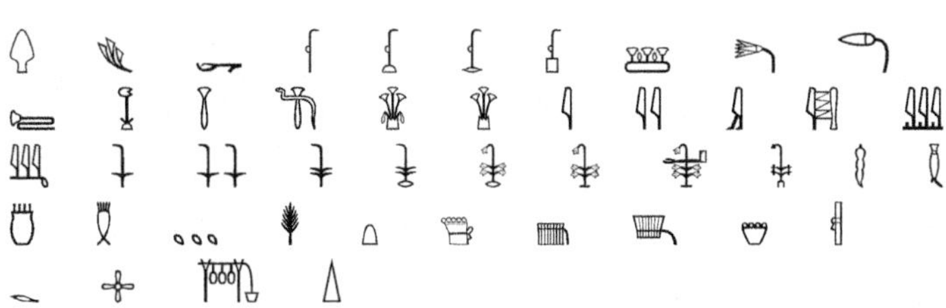

M1	**iAm**	tree	**tree, charm, favour**
M2	**Hn, is**	herb, flower	**vessel, tomb, chamber**
M3	**nxt, xt**	branch of wood	**wood, tree, strong**
M4	**rnpt**	palm branch no leaves	**be young, vigorous, year**
M5	**ti**	M4 and X1	**season**
M6	**tr, ri**	M4 and D21	**season, Egypt**
M7	**rnpi**	M4 and Q3	**be young, vigorous**
M8	**SA**	pool lotus flowers	**pool, meadow, appoint**
M9	**sSn**	lotus flower	**lotus**
M10	**nHbt**	lotus bud	**lotus bud**
M11	**(wADbw)**	flower on twisted stalk	**offer (wdn), shores**
M12	**xA**	lotus leaf stalk rhizome	**lotus plants, 1,000**
M13	**waD**	stem of papyrus	**papyrus column, be green**
M14	**wAD**	M13 and I10	**the sea, bequeath**
M15	**Ax**	clump of papyrus buds	**swamps, Chemmis**
M16	**Ha**	clump of papyrus	**would that! capture, Delta**
M17	**i**	flowering reed	**reeds,** phonetic sound **i**
M17*	**y**	two flowering reeds	phonetic sound **y**
M18	**ii**	M17 and D54	**come**
M19	**aAbt**	offering bundle	**offering, offering pile**
M20	**sxt**	reeds	**marsh country, peasant**
M21	**sm**	reeds with loop	**herb, plant, succour**

M22	**nxb**	rush with shoots	**germination, Nekhbet** (vulture goddess)
M22*	**nn**	two rushes shoots	**this, rushes**
M23	**swt**	plant of Upper Egypt	**plant, but**
M24	**rSw**	M23 and D21	**south**
M25	**rSw**	flowering M24	as M24
M26	**Sma**	flowering M23 planted	**chantress, singer**
M27	**Sma**	M26 and D36	as M26
M28	**mDw-Sma**	M26 and V20	**greatest of the tens of the South**
M29	**nDm**	sweet pod	**tree, sweet, pleasant**
M30	**bnr**	sweet root	**sweet**
M31	**rd**	rhizome of lotus	**grow**
M32	**rwd**	as M31	**be strong**
M33	**it**	grains of corn	**barley, corn, Nepri**
M34	**bty**	ear of emmer wheat	**emmer**
M35	**aHaw, wbn**	heap of cor	**heaps, overflow**
M36	**Dr**	bundle of flax	**since, hold fast**
M37	**Dr**	bundle of flax	as M36
M38	**dmA**	bundle of flax	**bind together**
M39	**rnpt**	basket of fruit or grain	**fruit, vegetables**
M40	**is**	tied reeds	**tomb, crew**
M41	**aS**	log of wood	**cedar**
M42	**wn**	flower	**cattle, be young, ea**
M43	**irp**	grape vine on sticks	**vine, wine, gardener**

M44 spd thorn **thorn, sharp**

N. Sky, Earth, Water

N1-N42

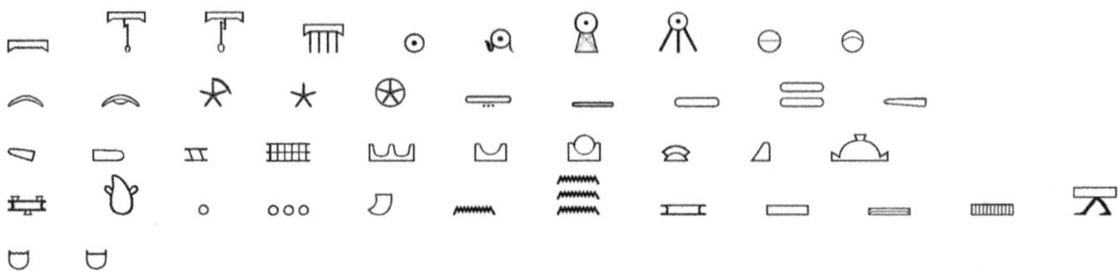

N1 **pt, Hry** sky, heavens **heaven, high, above**

N2 **grH** sky, lightning, power sceptre **night, darkness, dusk**

N3 use as N2

N4 **idt** rain from the sky **rain, dew, rain-storm**

N5 **ra, hrw** sun, day-time **sun, day, Ra (sun god)**

N6 **ra** sun with uraeus **sun**

N7 **Xrt-hrw** T28 under the sun **day-time, course of the day**

N8 **Axw, wbn** sunshine **sunshine, rise, shine**

N9 **psD** half moon **new-moon festival**

N10 crescent moon as N9

N11 **iaH** crescent moon **moon**

N12 **Abd** crescent moon, hidden disc **moon, month**

N13 **nt** five pointed star and N11 **half-moon festival**

N14 **sbA, dwA** five pointed star, Sirius **star, teach, adore**

N15 **dwAt** star in circle **underworld**

N16	**tA**	land, 3 grains sand	**earth, land**
N17		land	as N16
N18		sandy tract, foreign land	**island**
N19	**Hr-Axty**	Horus of the 2 hhorizons	**Ra-Harakti**
N20	**wDb**	long strip of land	**sand bank, shore**
N21	**tA**	short strip of land, angled	**bank, region, earth**
N22		O. K. form of N20 and N21	**field**
N23	**tAS**	irrigation canal	**land, boundary**
N24	**spAt**	land, irrigation canals	**district, nome**
N25	**xAst**	hill country	**foreign land, desert**
N26	**Dw**	mountains	**mountain, Abydos**
N27	**Axt**	sunrising over mountain	**horizon**
N28	**xA**	rising sun, rays	**sunrise, appear in glory**
N29	**q**	hill slope	**hill, height,** phonetic **q**
N30	**iAt**	mound shrubs	**mound**
N31	**wAt**	road shrubs	**road**
N32		lump of clay	**runners, clay, filthy**
N33	**Say**	grain of sand	**sand, metal**
N33*	-**w**	three grains sand	plural ending
N34	**xaw**	ignot of metal	**weapons, copper**
N35	**n**	water ripples	**water,** phonetic **n**
N35*	**mw**	three ripples of water	**water, wave, wash**
N36	**mr, mi**	canal	**canal, love, liver**
N37	**S**	garden pool	**pool,** phonetic **S**

N38	**S**	garden pool edges	as N37
N39	**S**	pool full of water	as N37
N40	**Sm**	pool and D54	**go**
N41	**Hm, idt**	well full of water	**well, pool, rescue, cow**
N42		as N41	

O. Buildings, Parts of Buildings etc

O1-O51

O1	**pr**	house, room, building	**house, building, room**
O2	**pr-HD**	white-house	**treasury, white house**
O3	**prt-Xrw**	House bread oar beer	**invocation offerings**
O4	**h**	field reed shelter	**room,** phonnetic **h**
O5	**mr**	winding wall	**street**
O6	**Hwt**	enclosure with shrine room	**temple, tomb**
O7		use as O6	
O8	**Hwt-Aat**	O7 and O29	**temple, castle**
O9	**nbt-Hyt**	O7 and V30	**Nephthys (goddess)**
O10	**Ht-Hr**	O6 and G5	**Hathor (goddess)**

O11	**aH**	palace with battlements	**palace**
O12	**H**	O11 and D36	use as O11
O13	**sbx**	battlements	**gateway, enclosure**
O14		half battlement	use as O13
O15	**wsxt**	walled enclosure	**hall in palace or temple**
O16	**tA**	gateway wit cobras	**curtain**
O17	**tA**	O.K. form of O16	use as O16
O18	**kAri**	shrine	**chapel, shrine**
O19	**pr-wr**	early shrine	**Great House**
O20	**xm**	shrine	**shrine, santuary**
O21	**sH-nTr**	facade of shrine	**divine-booth**
O22	**sH**	open booth on wadj pole	**booth, council**
O23	**Hb-sd**	dual booth used in sed-festival	**jubilee, sed-festival**
O24	**mr**	pyramid and wall enclosure	**pyramid, tomb**
O25	**txn**	obelisk	**obelisk**
O26	**wD**	stela	**stela, station**
O27	**xA**	hall of columns, office	**night**
O28	**iwn**	column	**column**
O29	**aA**	wooden column	**column, great**
O30	**sxnt**	forked pole	**support (of heaven)**
O30U	**abt**	forked pole upside down	**fork**
O31	**aA**	door	**door**
O32	**sbA**	gateway	**door, gateway**
O33	**srx** f	acade of palace or tomb	**banner - for Horus name**

O34	**s**	door bolt	**bolt,** phonetic s
O35	**sb**	bolt on D54	**go, pass, send, bring**
O36	**inb**	wall	**wall**
O37	**whn**	falling wall	**overthrow**
O38	**qnbt**	corner of wall	**corner, angle**
O39	**inr**	stonne slab, brick	**stone**
O40	**rwd**	stairway	**stairway**
O41	**qAy**	double stairway	**ascent, high place**
O42	**Ssp**	fence outside shrine	**receive, daylight**
O43	**Ssp**	O.K. form of O42	as O42
O44	**iAt**	temple of Min emblem	**rank, office**
O45	**ipt**	domed building	**harem**
O46	**ipt**	old form of O45	use as O45
O47	**nxn**	early building	**Hieraconpolis** (Nekhen)
O48	**nxn**	use as O47	
O49	**niwt**	town crossroads	**town**
O50	**sp**	threshing floor	**threshing floor, time**
O51	**Snwt**	heap of grain	**granary**

P. Ships and Parts of Ships

P1-P11

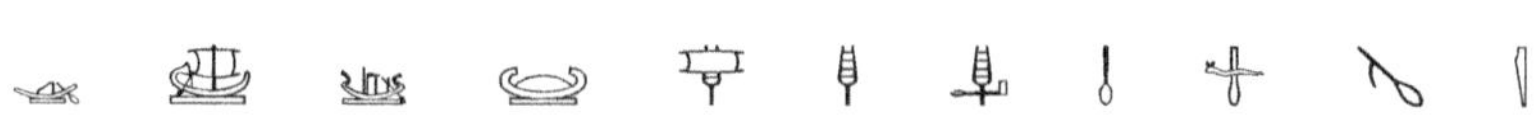

P1	**dpt, xdi**	boat on water	**ship, fare down stream**
P2	**xnti**	ship under sail	**sail upstream**
P3	**wiA**	sacred bark	**sacred bark**
P4	**wHa**	firshermen's boat	**fishermen**
P5	**TAw**	sail	**breath, wind**
P6	**aHa**	mast	**stand**
P7	**aHaw**	mast and D36	use as P6
P8	**xpt, xrw**	oar	**oar, voice**
P9	**xr-fy**	oar and I19	**says**
P10	**Hmw, Hmy**	steering oar	**steering oar, steersman**
P11	**mnit**	mooring post	**mooring post**

Q. Domestic annd Funerary Furniture

Q1-Q7

Q1	**st, Ast**	seat, throne	**seat, place, lap, jar, Isis**
Q2	**ws**	portable seat	**Osiris**
Q3	**p**	stool of reed mat	**base, seat,** phonetic **p**
Q4	**wsr**	head rest	**head-rest**
Q5	**hn**	chest	**box, chest**
Q6	**qrs**	coffin	**coffin, bury**
Q7	**xt, sDt**	flaming brazier	**fire, heat, cook**

R. Temple Furniture and Sacred Emblems

R1-R25

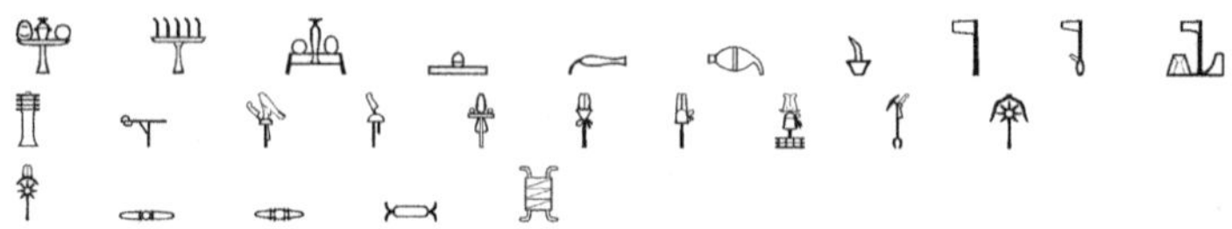

R1		**xAt**	offering table, loaves beer	**table of offerings**
R2		**xAy**	offering table, bread slices	**table of offerings**
R3		**wDHw**	table loaves vase	**table of offerings**
R4		**Htp**	loaf X2 on reed mat	**alter, rest, pleased**
R5		**kAp**	fumigation censer	**fumigate, harem, nursery**
R6		**kAp**	O.K. R5	as R5
R7		**snTr, bA**	incense bowl flame	**incense, soul, ram**
R8		**nTr**	flag pole	**god, divine**
R9		**bd**	R8 and V33	**natron**
R10		**Xr-nTr**	nTr sign plus T28 and N29	**necropolis**
R11		**Dd**	reed column	**column, be stable**
R12		**iAt**	standard, banner	**standard**
R13		**imnt**	falcon, banner, feather	**west, right, right hand**
R14		**imnt, wnmy**	banner, feather	**west, right hand**
R15		**iAbt**	spear standard	**east, left, left hand**
R16		**wx**	papyrus wand, feathers	**Banner of Cusae**
R17		**tA-wr**	plumes, banner, knot	**Abydos Nome, This**

R18 	**tA-wr**	R17 plus spAt N24	as R17
R19 	**wsr**	**was** sceptre, feather	**Thebes (Waset)**
R20 	**sSt**	banner, flower, horns	**Seshat (goddess)**
R21 	**sSt**	O.K. form of R20	as R20
R22	**mnw, xm**	god Min emblem	**Min (god), shrine**
R23	**mnw, xm**	O.K. form of R22	**Min (god), shrine**
R24 	**nt**	two bows	**Neith (goddess)**
R25 	**nt**	O.K. form of R24	**Neith (goddess)**

S. Crowns, Dress, Sceptres etc

S1-S45

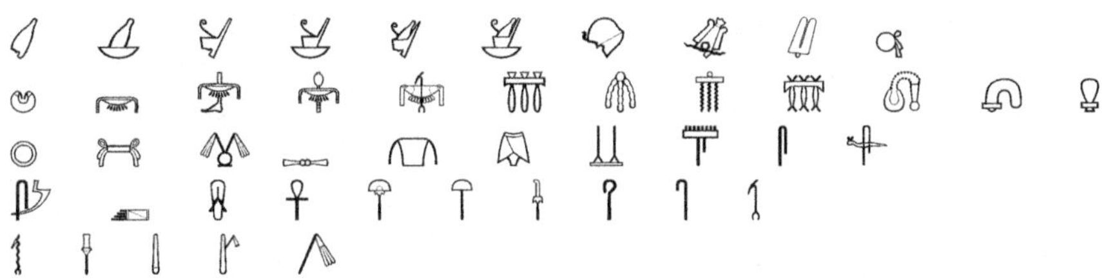

S1 	**HDt**	white crown Upper Egypt	**the white crown**
S2 	**wrrt**	white crown in basket	**great crown**
S3 	**dSrt**	red crown Lower Egypt	**the red crown**
S4 	**nt**	red crown in basket	**red crown**
S5 	**sxmty**	red and white crown	**the double crown**
S6 	**wrrt**	double crown in basket	**great crown**
S7 	**xprS**	blue war crown	**blue crown**

Code	Sign	Transliteration	Description	Meaning
S8		**Atf**	atef crown, two plumes	**atef crown**
S9		**Swty**	two plumes	**double plumes**
S10		**wAHw**	headband	**wreath**
S11		**wsx**	broad collar	**collar, breadth**
S12		**nbyt, nbw, Hd**	bead collar	**collar, gold, silver**
S13		**nbi**	bead collar and D58	**gild, fasion**
S14		**HD**	bead collar and mace T3	**silver**
S14A		**Dam**	bead collar and S40	**electrum**
S15		**THn**	pectoral of glass beads	**faience, glass, sparkle**
S16		**THnt**	as S15	**faience, glass**
S17		**THnt**	as S15	
S17A		**Ssmt**	sacred girdle	**sacred girdle, malachite**
S18		**mnit**	nnecklace counter weight	**bead necklace, menit**
S19		**sD-Awty**	necklace cylinder seal	**treasurer**
S20		**xtm**	cylinder seal	**seal**
S21			ring	**ring (iwaw, aaw)**
S22		**sT,stt**	shoulder not	**Asia**
S23		**dmd, dmD**	two flagella, shen ring	**unit**
S24		**Tst, Ts**	girdle knot	**knot, tie, bind**
S25		**iAa, aw**	garment with ties	**skirt, dragoman (interpreter)**
S26		**Sndyt**	kilt	**kilt**
S27		**mnxt**	clothe two fringes	**clothing**
S28		**Hbs**	senet board Y5 and strips of clothe	**clothe, clothing**
S29		**s**	folded clothe	phonetic **s**

S30	**sf**	S29 and I9	**yesterday**
S31	**smA**	S29 and U1	**fighting bull**
S32	**siA**	clothe with fringe	**piece of clothe, recognize**
S33	**Tbt**	sandal	**sandal, be shod**
S34	**anx**	sandal strap	**sandal strap, mirror, live**
S35	**iwt**	sunshade, ostrich feathers	**shadow, shade**
S36	**iwt**	O.K. form of A35	
S37	**xw**	fan	**fan**
S38	**HqA, Awt**	crook	**sceptre, rule, goats**
S39	**awt**	peasant's crook	**crook, flocks**
S40	**wAs, iAtt**	sceptre, Seth head	**was-sceptre, milk**
S41	**Dam**	sceptre, spiral shaft	**sceptre, fine gold**
S42	**abA, sxm**	sceptre of authority	**sceptre, stela, power**
S43	**md**	walking stick	**stick, staff, speak**
S44	**Ams**	stick and flagellum	**sceptre**
S45	**nxAxA**	flagellum (flail, fly-swot)	**flagellum**

T. Warefare, Hunting, Butchery

T1-T35

T1	**mnw**	prehistoric mace	**mace**
T2	**sqr**	striking mace	**smite**
T3	**HD**	mace, pear shaped head	**mace, be bright, white**
T4	**HD**	mace with hand strap	as T3
T5	**HD**	mace and I10	as T3
T6	**HDDwt**	mace with two I10's	**brightness (doubly bright)**
T7	**mDH**	axe	**hew, carpenter**
T7A	**AqHw**	axe	**axe**
T8	**tpy**	ancient dagger	**chief**
T8A	**bA-gsw**	M.K. dagger	**dagger**
T9	**pD**	bow of oryx horn	**bow, stretch**
T10	**iwnt**	composite bow	**bow**
T11	**sin,**	arrow	**perish, snw: physician, swn: arrow**
T12	**rwD**	bow string	**bow string, sandstone**
T13	**rs**	lashed wood sticks	**be wakeful, vigilant**
T14	**amaA**	throw stick	**throw stick, throw**
T15	**amaA**	use as T14	
T16	**xpS**	scimetar	**scimetar**
T17	**wrrt**	chariot	**chariot**
T18	**Sms**	crook and attachement	**follow, accompany**
T19	**qs**	harpoon head of bone	**bone, harpoon, bury**
T20	**qs**	O.K. form of T19	as T19
T21	**wa**	barbed harpoon	**one**
T22	**sn**	harpoon	**two, brother, smell, kiss**

T23		**sn**	harpoon	as T22
T24		**iH, aHt**	fishing net	**to net, field, holding**
T25		**DbA**	reed floats	**floats, adorn, replace**
T26		**sxt**	bird trap	**trap, snare**
T27		**sxt**	O.K.form of T26	as T26
T28		**Xr**	butcher's block	**under, storehouse**
T29		**nmt**	T28 and T30	**place of slaughter**
T30		**ds, dm**	knife	**knife, be sharp, cut**
T31		**sSm**	knife sharpener	**guide, lead**
T32		**sSm**	T31 with D54	as T31
T33		**sSm**	knife sharpener	**butcher**
T34		**nm**	butcher's knife	**knife, orphan, friend**
T35		**nm**	as T34	

U. Agriculture, Crafts, and Professions

U1-U41

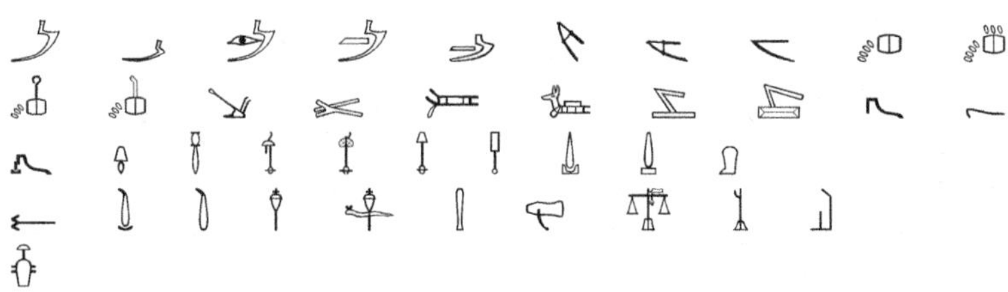

U1		**mA**	sickle	**see**
U2		**mA**	as U1	**see**
U3		**mAA**	U1 and D4	**see**

U4	**mAat**	U1 and Aa11	**truth**
U5	**mAat**	as U4	**truth**
U6	**ad, mr**	hoe	**hack up, cultivate, love**
U7	**ad, mr**	as U6	
U8	**Hn**	hoe without joining rope	**hoe, Hnw-bark**
U9	**bdt, xAi**	corn measure, grain	**emmer, corn, measure**
U10	**it**	U9 and M33	**barley, corn**
U11	**HqAt**	U9 and S38	**HqAt-corn measure**
U12	**HqAt**	U9 and D50	**HqAt-corn measure**
U13	**hb, Sna**	plough	**ebony, repel**
U14	**Sna**	joined branches of wood	as U13
U15	**tm, itm**	sledge	**sledge, perish, Atum (god)**
U16	**wnS, biA**	sledge, jackal head	**sledge, copper, wonder**
U17	**grg**	excavating tool	**found, extablish, lie**
U18	**grg**	O.K. form of U17	as U17
U19	**nw**	adze	phonogram **nw**
U20	**nw**	O.K. form of U19	as U19
U21	**stp**	cutting adze	**cut up, choose**
U22	**mnx**	chisel	**fashion, carve, chisel**
U23	**mr**	chisel	**be ill, friennd, courtier**
U24	**Hmt**	weighted stone drill	**craft, art**
U25	**Hmt**	O.K. form of U24	**craft, art**
U26	**wbA**	drill boring hole in bead	**open up**

U27	**wbA**	O.K.form of U26	**open up**
U28	**DA**	fire-drill	**fire drill, ferry across**
U29	**DA**	O.K. form of U28	as U28
U30	**tA**	potter's kiln	**kiln, be hot, difficult**
U31	**rtH**	baking instrument	**baker, restrain, prison**
U32	**sHm, smn**	pestle and mortar	**pound, natron**
U33	**ti, t**	pestle	**pestle, you are, may she**
U34	**xsf**	spindle	**spin, rebel, oppose**
U35	**xsf**	U34 and I9	as U34
U36	**Hm**	fuller's club	**fuller, slave, Majesty**
U37	**Xaq**	razor	**shave**
U38	**mnxt**	balance	**balance**
U39	**wTs**	upright of balance	**post, lift, carry**
U40	**wTsw**	semi-hieratic form of U39	**those who have worn**
U41	**tx**	plummet for balance	**plummet**

V. Rope, Fibre, Baskets, Bags etc

V1-V39

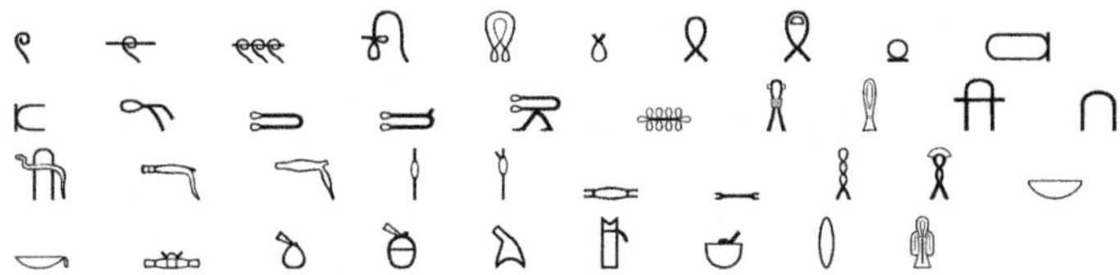

V1	**nwH, Snt**	coil of rope	**rope, dispute, content**
V2	**sTA**	V1 and O34	**drag, draw, aroura**
V3	**sTAw**	V2 with 3 cords	**necropolis**
V4	**wA**	lasso	**lasso, far, place, endure**
V5	**snT**	looped rope	**plan, plot out**
V6	**Ss**	cord	**cord, rope, alabaster**
V7	**Sni, Sn**	inverted loop	**encircle, tree, repel**
V8	**Sni, Sn**	as V7	
V9	**Snw**	origin of cartouche	**cartouche**
V10	**Snw, rn**	cartouche	**circuit, name**
V11	**dni**	half cartouche	**dam off, restrain**
V12	**sSd, arq**	string or linen	**headband, swear**
V13	**T**	tethering rope	**fetterer,** phonetic **T**
V14	**Tsi**	V13 with tick	**lift**
V15	**iti**	V13 and D54	**seize**
V16	**sA**	looped cord	**hobble, protection**
V17	**sA**	papyrus loop	**protection**
V18	**sA**	O.K. form of V17 as V17	
V19	**mDt, TmA**	cattle hobble	**stable, public registry**
V20	**mD**	hobble no bar	**stables**
V21	**mD, TmA**	V20 and I10	**stables, registry**

V22		**mH**	whip	**fill**
V23		**mH**	O.K. V22	as V22
V24		**wD**	cord wound stick	**command**
V25		**wD**	as V24	
V26		**aD, ad**	netting needle	**spool, reel, be safe**
V27		**aD, ad**	O.K.form of V26 as V26	
V28		**H, Hat**	twisted flax	**wick,** phonetic **H**
V29		**Sk, wAH**	swab	**wipe, perish, place**
V30		**nbt, nb**	wicker basket	**basket, lord, every, all**
V31		**k**	basket with handle	phonetic **k**
V32		**gAw**	wicker work bundle	**bundles, be narrow**
V33		**sSr**	bag of linen	**linen, clothe, thing, corn**
V34		**sSr**	as V33	
V35		**sSr**	O.K. form of V34 as V34	
V36		**Hn**	receptacle	**occupations, period, end**
V37		**idr**	bandage	**bandage, bind, herd**
V38		**wt**	bandage, O.K.	**bandage, mummy cloth**
V39			**tie** amulet	**amulet**

W. Vessels of Stone and Earthenware

W1-W25

W1	**mrHt**	sealed oil jar	**oil, ungent, ointment**
W2	**bAs**	oil jar	**jar, Bastet (city)**
W3	**SS, Hb**	alabaster bowl	**alabaster, feast, mourn**
W4	**Hb**	W3 and O22	**feast**
W5	**Xry-Hbt**	W3 and T28	**lector priest**
W6	**wHt**	O.K. vessel sign	**cauldron**
W7	**mAt**	granite bowl	**red granite, proclaim**
W8	**Abt**	form of W7	**family**
W9	**Xnm**	stone jug handle	**join, Khnum**
W10	**iab**	cup	**cup, unite**
W11	**nst, g**	jar stand	**seat,** phonetic **g**
W12	**nst, g**	jar stand	as W11
W13	**dSrt**	red pot	as W11, **red-pot**
W14	**Hst, Hs**	water jar	**water jar, praise**
W15	**qbb, qbH**	water jar, water	**cool, libate**
W16	**qbHw**	W15 and W12	**libation**
W17	**xnt**	rack of 3 water jars	**racks, in front of**
W18	**xnt**	O.K. 4 water jars as W17	
W19	**mr, mi**	milk jug, carrying net	**milk jug, like**
W20	**irTt**	milk jug	**milk**

W21	**irp**	two wine jars	**wine**
W22	**Hnqt**	beer jug	**beer**
W23	**qrHt**	jug with handles	**beer**
W24	**nw, in**	pot	**council, Nekhebet**
W25	**ini**	pot and D54	**bring, fetch**

X. Loaves and Cakes

X1-X8

X1	**t**	bread	**bread,** phonetic **t**
X2	**t**	bread	**bread**
X3	**t**	bread	as X2
X4	**sn**	roll of bread	**bread, food**
X5	**sn**	hieratic X4	as X4
X6	**pAt**	round marked loaf	**loaf, antiquity**
X7	**wAb**	half loaf	**food, eat**
X8	**di**	conical loaf	**give**

Y. Writings, Games, Music

Y1-Y8

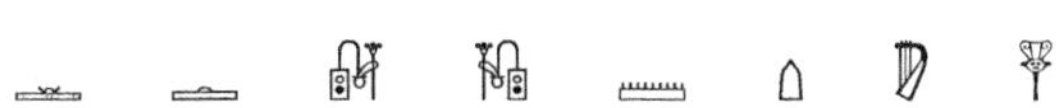

Y1	**mDAt**	papyrus scroll	**papyrus scroll,** abstract
Y2	**mDAt**	O.K.form Y1	as Y1
Y3	**sS**	scribe's apparatus	**scribe, writings**
Y4	**sS**	reversed Y3	as Y3
Y5	**mn**	senet board	**remain**
Y6	**ibA**	senet game piece	**senet game piece, dance**
Y7	**bnt**	harp	**harp**
Y8	**sSSt, sxm**	sistrum	**sistrum**

Z. Strokes, Signs from Hieratic, Geometrical Figures

Z1-Z11

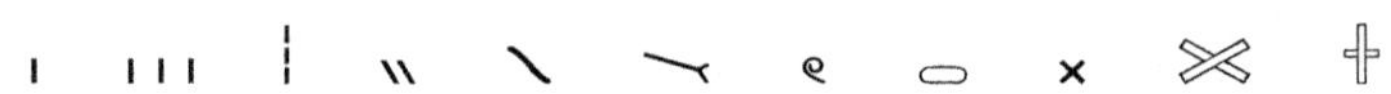

Z1	**wa**	single stroke	**one, unit**
Z2	**w, t**	three strokes	**plural ending**
Z3	**w**	three strokes	**plural ending**
Z4	**i, y**	two diagonal strokes	**dual ending**
Z5		curved hieratic stroke	substitute for difficult signs
Z6	**mt, xft**	hhieratic for A13&14	**die, enemy**
Z7	**w**	hieratic for G45	phonetic **w**
Z8	**Snnw**	oval ring	**circuit, round**
Z9	**HDi, DAi**	crossed sticks	**damage, cross**

Z10	**HDi, DAi**	O.K. Z9	as Z9
Z11	**imy, imi**	crossed planks	**who is in, not be**

Aa. Unclassified

Aa1-Aa31

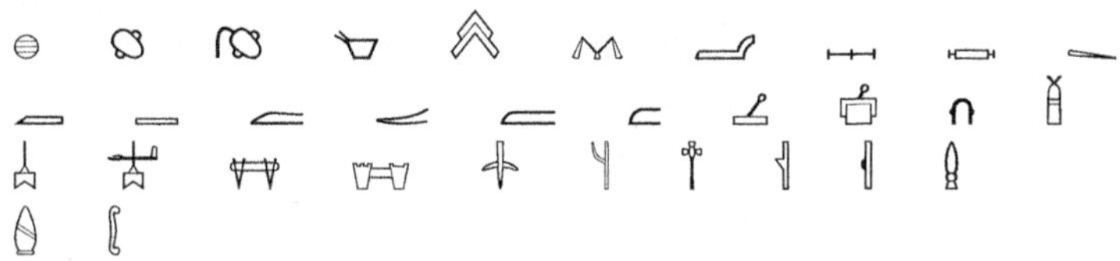

Aa1	**x**	placenta	**placenta,** phonetic **x**
Aa2	**Sfw, wt**	gland	**growths, embalmer**
Aa3	**wsSt, sT**	Aa2 with liquid	**urine, odour**
Aa4	**bA**	pot	as W10 **cup, unite**
Aa5	**Htp, Hp**	steering gear of ship	**proceed by boat, Hepy**
Aa6	**tmA, TmA**	double flail	**mat, cadaster**
Aa7	**sqr**	unknown	**smite**
Aa8	**DAtt**	irrigation runnels	**estate, magistrate**
Aa9	**xwd**	unknown	**rich**
Aa10	**drf**	unknown	**writing**
Aa11	**mAa**	unknown	**truth**
Aa12	**mAa**	O.K.form Aa11	as Aa11
Aa13	**im**	unknown	**give**
Aa14	**im**	O.K. form Aa13	**give**
Aa15	**im**	as Aa13	**give**

Aa16	𓐞	**gs**	short Aa13	**half, side**
Aa17	𓐟	**sA**	back of	**back**
Aa18	𓐠	**sA**	later form of Aa17	**back**
Aa19	𓐡	**Hr**	unknown	**prepare**
Aa20	𓐢	**apr**	unknown	**provide, equip**
Aa21	𓐣	**wDa, StX**	carpenter's tool	**sever, judge, Seth**
Aa22	𓐤	**wDa, Stx**	Aa21 and D36	as Aa21
Aa23	𓐥	**mDd**	warp between posts	**hit, adhere**
Aa24	𓐦	**mDd**	O.K. form Aa23	as Aa23
Aa25	𓐧	**smA**	unknown	**priest's title**
Aa26	𓐨	**sbi**	like T14	**rebel**
Aa27	𓐩	**nD**	unknown	**ask, enquire**
Aa28	𓐪	**qd**	bricklayer's instrument	**build, fashion**
Aa29	𓐫	**qd**	O.K. form Aa28	as Aa28
Aa30	𓐬	**Xkr**	wall frieze	**be adorned, ornnament**
Aa31	𓐭	**Xkr**	as Aa30	
Aa32	𓐮	**TA-St**	bow	**Nubia**

EGYPTIAN VOCABULARY

Vocabulary Index

Egyptian Vocabulary

The order: Sign, Phonetic Sound, Gardiner's Code, Meaning.

 **A**

	**A**	A	the phonetic sign **A**
	**At**	A-t:N5	**moment, instant**
	**At**	A-t:F9-N5:Z1	**moment, moment of rage**
	**Aw**	Aw-w	**length (of space, time), long, extended**
	**Aw**	Aw-w-D41	**length (of space)**
	**Aw**	Aw-w-t:Y1	**length (of space, time), complete, entire**
	**Aw**	Aw-A14	**desceased**
	**Aw**	Aw-Y1v	**long (space, time)**
	**Aw**	A-h-w-G37-A1	**needy person**
	**Awt**	Aw-w-t:T30	**long knife**
	**Awt-a**	Aw-w:t-a:Z1-Y1:Z2	**gifts**
	**Awy**	Aw-w-i-i-A24	**extend, present, announce, arouse**
	**Awy**	Aw-Z7:D40	**extend (arm)**
	**Awy-drt**	Aw-w-i-i-A24-d:t-Z1	**lay hands on**
	**AwH**	Aw-w-H-A24	**do violence**
	**Awt**	Aw-t:Y1:Z2	**oblations**
	**Awt**	Aw-w-t:X4:N33*N33*N33	**offering gifts**

Awt	Aw-t-w-N18	**gifts**
Awt	Aw-t-w-Y1:Y1:Y1	**length (of time)**
Awt	Aw:X1-X2-X6-W22	**gifts, food**
Awta	Aw-t-w-a:Z1-Y1:Z2	**gift**
Awt-ib	Aw-t*F34:Y1	**happiness**
Ab	Ab-b-D54	**stop**
s-Ab	z-Ab-Y1	**cause to tarry**
Abi	Ab-b-A2	**to long, desire, wish**
Aby	Ab-b-i-i-E24	**panther, leopard**
Aby	E24	**panther, leopard**
Abw	Ab-b-w-E26	**elephant**
Abw	Ab-b-w-W7:N25	**Elephantine (First Cataract island)**
Abw	Ab-w-W8:O49	**Elephantine (First Cataract island)**
Abw	Ab-b-w-Q7	**to brand**
Abx	Ab-b-x:t-Z9:Y1	**to mix, mingle, join, unite**
Abxt	Ab-b-x:t-Z9:a-W22:Z2	**a liquid, solution**
Abt	**Ab-b-t-A1-B1-Z3**	**family kindred**
Abt	Ab-b-t:W8-A1*B1:Z2	**family kindred**
Abd	N11:sbA-d:N5*Z1	**month**
Abd	N11	**month**
AbDw	Ab-N25-b	**Abydos**
AbDw	Ab-b-N26:O49	**Abydos**
Apd	A-p:d-G39	**bird**
Afa	A-f:a-E28	**be greedy, greed**

Am	A-m-Q7	**to burn up**
Ami	A-mi-i-A24	**mix, compound**
Amm	A-m-m-D49	**seize, grip**

Ammt: grasp

Ams	A-ms-s-S44	**a royal sceptre or staff**
Ar	A-r:T12-A24	**restrain, hold back**
Ahw	A-h-w-G37	**pain, trouble**
Ahd	A-h-d:G37	**feeble, faint**
AHt	A-H-t:N23	**field**
Ax	Ax-x:Y1	**good, useful, beneficial, glorious**
Ax	G25-Z1	**blessed spirit**
Ax	Ax-x-A51	**spirit (of the deceased)**
Axt	Ax-x:t-I13	**uraeus (serpent on royal crown)**
Axw	Ax-w-Y1:Z2	**skills, expertise, craft**
Axw	A-x-w-N8	**sunshine**
Axw	N8-w-A40	**sunshine**
Axt	M8:x*t	**inundation (season)**
Axt	Axt:t*Z1	**horizon**
Axt	N27:t*O1	**horizon**
Axt	Ax-x*t:N18	**horizon**
Axt	N27:t*O1	**tomb**
Axt	M8:x-t:N5	**inundation season**
Axt	M8:x*t	**inundation season**
Axt	A-x:t-I13	**royal uraeus**

Axt	A-x:t-D5	**the Beneficient one (eye of Ra)**
Axty	M8:x-t*y:N5	**of the inundation season**
Axty	Axt:N27	**who is from the horizon**
Axty	N18:N18	**who is from the horizon**
AXa	A-X:a-D51:D40	**to scratch**
As	A-s-V2:D54	**hasten, overtake, hurry, flow fast, quickly**
As	A-s-Aa2	**bald, viscera**
Asx	A-z:x-T30	**reap**
Ast	st-t-B1	**Isis (goddess)**
Ast	F51:t-B1	**Isis (goddess)**
ASr	A-S:r-Q7	**roast**
Aq	A-q:G37	**perish**
Aqi	A-q-G37	**to perish**
AqHw	A-q-H-w-T7A	**axe**
Aqs	A-q-s-V60?	**Akes, a divinity of the royal apparel**
Aqs	S38-s-V18	**Akes, a divinity of the royal apparel**
Aqs	A-q-s-V6	**a type of garment**
Akr	A-k:r-A40	**Aker, an earth god, the earth**
At	A-t-A24	**to be white, to be pale**
Atp	A-t:p-A9	**to load**
Atf	A-t:f-S8	**the Atef crown**
ATp	A-T:Q3	**to load**
ATp	A-T:p-A9-A24	**load**
ATp, Atp	A9-a	to **load**

	**ATpw**	A-T:p-A9-Y1:Z2	**load**
	**Ad**	A-d:I3	**to be aggressive, savage**
	**Ad**	A-d:D54	**weak, listless**

𓇋 i

Transliteration	Signs	Meaning
i	i-A2	**O (you)!**
i	i	**say**
.i	A1	suffix pronoun: **I, me, my**
Variations:	G7, A40, A42, i-A1	
i	i-Z1-M2	**reed**
iAAt	i-A-A-t:M3	**branch**
iAw	N30-N21:Z2	**ruins**
iAAw	i-A-A-M2-Z3	**reeds**
iAAt	i-A-A-t:M3	**stick**
iAw	i-A-w-A19	**old age**
iAw	i-A30	**praise**
iAw	i-A-A30	**praise**
iAw	A30-w-Y1:Z2	**praise**
iAwt	i-A-Z7:t-O44-Y1:Z2	**office, function, profession**
iAwy	i-A-Z7:y-A19-Y1	**old age**
iAwy	A19	**old age**
iAby	iAb-b	**left, left hand**
iAbty	iAb-b-t:y	**eastern, eaterner**
iAbtt	iAb-b-t*t:N25	**the East**
iAbtt	iAb-b-t*t:N25	**the East**
iAm	M1-m-O1	**tent**
iAdr	i-A-d:r-V37-E1:Z2	**herd**

	**iArw**	i-A-r-w-M2-M2-M2	**reeds**
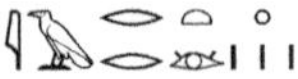	**iArrt**	i-A-r:r-t:D5-N33:Z2	**grapes**
	**irrt, iArrt**	i-ir:r:t-M43	**wine**
	**iArrt**	i-A-r:r:t-D5:N33*Z2	**grapes**
	**iAx, iAxi**	i-A-x-M15	**be inundated**
	**iAs**	i-A-s-A28	**bald**
	**iAS**	i-A-S-A2	**to call out, to summon**
	**iAqt**	i-A-q:t-M2-Z3	**vegetables, greens, leeks**
	**iAkb**	i-A-k-b-D3	**mourning, wailing**
	**iAt**	i-A-t:F37	**back**
	**iAt**	O44-t*Z1:Y1	**office (position), duty, function)**
	**iAt**	O44-O44-O44	**office (position), duty, function)**
	**iAt**	iAt-t:O1	**mound**
	**iAt**	i-A-t:N30-N21:Z1	**mound**
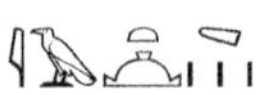	**iAt**	i-A-t:N30-N21:Z2	**ruins**
	**iAt**	N30:t*Z1	**mound**
	**iAt**	i-A-t:R12	**standard, banner, supporting religious symbols**
	**iAt**	i-A-t:F37	**back**
	**iAt**	F37-t:Z1	**back**
	**ii**	ii-i-D54	**to come, arrive, return**
	**iAb**	i-a:W10-b	**join together, unite**
	**iAm**	M1-m-M1	**a type of tree**
	**iAm**	M1-m-Y1v	**gracious, charming**
	**iAtt**	S40-t:t-W22	**milk, cream**

	**iAkb**	i-A-k-b-D3	**mourn**
	**iAT**	i-A-T-D57	**be mutilated, missing**
	**iAdt**	i-A-d:t*Z5-V1	**net**
	**iaA, iAa**	i-a-A	**skirt**
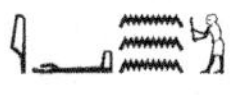	**ia, iai**	i-a-n:n:n-A24	**wash**

iai-ib: slake ones' desire, appetite, wrath

	**iab**	i-a:W10-b	**cup**
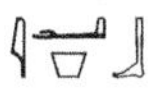	**iab**	i-a:W10-b	**unite**
	**ian**	i-a:n-E32	**baboon**
	**ianw**	i-a:n-nw-w-A2	**lamentation, sorrow, woe**
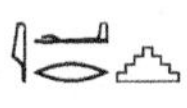	**iar**	i-a:r-O41	**ascend, mount up, approach**
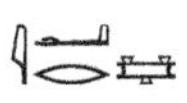	**iar**	i-a:r-N31	**ascend, mount up, approach**
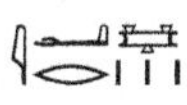	**iarw**	i-a:r-N31:Z2	**neigbourhood**
	**iart**	i-a:r:t-I12	**uraeus (protective serpent)**
	**iaH**	i-a-H-C9	**moon, moon god**
	**iaH**	i-a-H-N11\R90	**moon**
	iaH	N11	**moon**
	**iaH**	N12-G7	**moon, moon god**
	**iw**	ii-w	**to come, arrive, return**
	**iw**	D54-w	**come**
	**ii**	M18-i-D54	**come, welcome**
	**ii.ti**	ii-i-D54-ti-i	**welcome!**
	**iyt**	ii-i-i-t:G37:Z2	**harm, mishap, incident, trouble**
	**iw**	i-w	**behold (starts a sentence)**

iw	N18:N23*Z1	**island**
iw	E9-w-E14	**dog**
iwsnb	D54-w-s-n:b-A1	**Iusonbu (man's name)**
iw	E9:Z7-G37	**crime, wrongdoing, injustice**
iwyt	E9-w-i-i-t:G37:Z2	**wrongdoing**
iw	E9-w-A2	**complaint**
iwA	i-wA-E1	**ox**
iwy	E9-w-P1	**one without a boat**
iwyt	E9-w-i-i-t:O1	**street**
iwa	E9:a-F44:Z1	**thigh (of beef), femur**
iwa	E9:a-F44	**inherit**

iwat, iwaat: heritage, inheritance; iwaw: heir

iwa	E9-w-a:Y1	**inherit**
iwa	E9:a	**heir**
iwayt	E9:a-i-i-t-A1:Z2	**garrison, soldiery**
iwaw	E9-w-a:w-S21	**ring**
aaw	a:a-w-S21	**ring**
iwat	E9-a:t*Z5-Y1:Z2	**inheritance**
iwaw	E9-w-a-w-A1	**heir**
iwf	i-Z7:f-F51:Z2	**meat, flesh**
iwms	i-w-ms-s	**exageration**
iwn	i-E9:n-D3	**colour, complexion, nature**
iwn	O28-Z1	**column**

iwny iwn-n:y-O49 **Armant, Hermonthis, a town in Upper Egypt**

iwn-mwt.f iwn-Z1-mwt-t:f-A40 **Pillar of His Mother (Horus)**

iwnw iwn-nw:O49 **Heliopolis**

iwnw-Smaw iwn-nw:O49-M27-w-O49 **On of Upper Egypt (Thebes), lit. Southern Pillar Town**

iwnyt iwn-iwn-iwn-t:O1 **hall of columns**

iwnt iwn-T9:t-A14 **desert Nubian**

iwnt iwn-t:Z1 **bow**

iwnt iwn-n:t-O49 **Denderah, Tentyra, a town in Upper Egypt**

iwnt, Iwnty-Sty iwn-T10\R90-t-A13 **Nubian, foreigner, bowman**

iwnyt iwn-n-i-i-t:O49 **Esna, Latopolis, a town in U.E.**

iwr E9-Z7-wr:r-B3 **to conceive (a child), become pregnant**

iwh E9-w-h-D41:D40 **to load**

iwH E9-w-n:n:n-A24 **water, irrigate**

iwH E9-w-H-n:n:n-nw-A24 **to moisten**

iwsw E9-Z7-sw-Z7-xt **scales, balance**

iwty D35:t*y-G37 **which is not**

iwtyw D35:t*Z7-G37 **one who is not**

iwtn E9:t-n:N21*Z1 **ground, floor**

iwytt D35:t*t **that which does not exist**

ntt-iwtt n:t*t-D35:t*t **absolutely everything**

iwd E9-w-d:D54 **to separate (x from y), push off**

iwdnb D54-w-d:n-b-N33:Z2 **type of incense**

ib ib:Z1 heart, mind

ib i-b-E8-F27 kid, a young goat

ib i-b-E8 to think, suppose, imagine

ib i-b-A32 to dance

ib i-b-Y6 to dance

ibi i-b-E8-i-W7 laudanum (aromatic resin)

ibi i-b-E8-n:n:n-A2 to be thirsty, ibt: thirst

ibw i-b-E8-w-O1 refuge

ibnw i-b-n:nw*w-N33:Z2 alum

ibr i-R7-bA-r:Z1-E6 stallion

ibhty i-b-h-t:y-O39 stone used for beads

ibH i-b-H-F18 tooth

ip i-p:Y1 allot, to count, assess, acounting, calculate

ipwty, wpwty wp:p-t:Z9-D54-A1 messenger

ipw i-p-w that (mas.)

iptw i-p:t-w that (fem.)

ipn i-p:n this (mas.)

iptn i-p*t:n this (fem.)

ipt i-p:t-Q1-t:Z2-O49 Karnak, 'Most select of Places'

ipt-swt i-p:t-st-st-st-t:O49 Ipet-suit, 'Most select of Places' name of the temple at Karnak

ipt i-p:t-U9 a measure of capacity = 4 HqAt = 18 litres

ipt, wpt wp-t:Z9-A2 message, mission, occupation

ipt	i-p:t-O45	**harim, private apartments**
ipt	O15	**harim, private apartments**
ipt	O45-t:O1	**harim, private apartments**
if	i-f:F51	**meat**
ifd	i-f:d-D54	**to flee**
ifd	i-f:d-O39	**sheet, rectangular piece of cloth**
ifdy	i-f:d-y:a-S28	**a cloth, a square of cloth**
ifdt	i-f:d-t:Z2	**a four, quartet**
im	i-m	**there, therein, therewith, therefrom**
imA	i-mA-A-M1	**gracious, charming**
imAt	i-mA-t-M1	**charm, kindliness, graciousness**
imAw	M1-m-pr-w	**tent**
imy	Z11-m-y	**which is in,** var.
imy-ib	i-imi-ib:Z1	**favourite**
imy-wrt	imi-m-y-wr:r:t	**west side**
imyw-bAh	imi-m-D53-Z3	**who are in the presence of, those who lived before**
imyt-pr	imi-m:t-Y1:Z2-pr:Z1	**transfer of title to an estate**
imy-r	m:r	**overseer, superintendant**
imy-r	F20	**overseer, superintendant**
imy-r-pr	m-r:pr	**overseer of the house, steward**
imy-r-pr-wr	m-r:pr-A19	**chief steward**
imy-r-smyw-iAbtywt	m:r-N25:N25:N25-R15-b-r*t:N25	**overseer of the eastern deserts**

imy-r-rn.f imi-m-r:n:f-A1:Z2 **list of names**

imy-HAt imi-m-HAt:t*Z1 **former, previous, which/who was before, of olden times**

imy-HAt imi-m-HAt:t*Z1-A50-Z3 **those of former times, ancestors, predecessors**

imy-xt i-imi-m-xt:x*t-D54 **one who will come after, those of later times, future generations**

imy-sA imi-V17-A1 **attendant**

imi i-m-Aa15:D38 **give, put, cause**

imi i-m-D35 **'to do not'**

imi i-im-m-A2 **mourn**

imi-tw imi-m-y:t-w **between, between x and y**

imAx F39:Z1 **honour, veneration**

imAx i-mA:x-F39:Z1 **spinal chord**

iAx F39:Z1-F51 **spinal cord**

imAx i-mA:x-F39:Z1 **venerated state**

iAx F39:Z1-F51 **vein**

imAxy i-imAx:x-i-i-A50 **one who is honoured**

imw i-Aa15-m-P1:Z1 **boat**

imn i-mn:n:Y1 **hide**

imn i-mn:n-A40 **the god Amun**

imn-m-HAt <-i-mn:n-m-HAt-> **Amun-em-hat**

imn-nxt i-mn:n-n:xt:x*t-A24-A1 **Amun-nakhet**

imn R14 **right hand**

imnt R14-t:N25 **the west**

Transliteration	Code	Meaning
imnty	R14-t*y:N25	western
imr	i-mr:r-F21	to be deaf
imHt	i-Aa15:m-H-t:O1	cavern
in	i:n	by, through, so says
in	i-in:n-D54	to delay
int	i-in:n-t:N25	valley
int	i-n:t-in	bulti fish
im-m	i:n-m:a	who?
ini	W25:n	to bring, get, acquire, to attain, reach
inw	W25-nw:Z2	tribute, gifts, goods
intf	ini-t:f	Intef (man's name)
inb	in:n-b-O36	wall
inpw	i-n:p-w-E15-G7	Inpw (Anubis)
inm	i-K1:n-T34-m-F27	colour, skin
innw	i-A2-n:n:Z2	we, belongs to us
innw	i-nw:n:Z2	we, belongs to us
inr	i-n:r-O39	stone
inH	i-in:n-H-D13:D13	eyebrow(s)
inH	i-in:n-H-V1:D40	surround, enclose
inHrt	W25:n-H-Hr:r-t:N31	Onuris, the god of This N. of Abydos
inHrt	W25-N31	Onuris, the god of This
inHrt	W25:N1	Onuris, the god of This
inst	i-in:n-s-t-D56	shank

inq	i-n:q-D32:D40	**embrace, envelop**
ink	nw:k	**I, belongs to me**
ink	nw:k	**I, belongs to me**
ind	i-in:n-d:G37	**earlier**
inD	i-in:n-d:G37	**be ill, illness**
inD-Hr	i-Aa27-D-Hr*Z1	**hail to**
ir	i-r	**As for..., with respect to, toward**
ir-m-xt	i-r-m-xt:x*t-D54	**Now, after, now later, now afterwards, If...**
iry	i-r:y	**thereto, connected to, associated with, its, their, as to**
iry	i-r-A49	**he who is at, who pertains to**
iry	i-r:y-A49-Y1	**duty**
ir	i-r	**thereto, connected to, associated with, its, their, as to**
irw	i-r:w	**thereto, connected to, associated with, its, their, as to**
im-st-iry	m-Q1-O1:t-i-r:y	**in their proper place, in good order**
iry	i-r:A1	**companion, associate**
iry-aA	i-r:y-A48-aA:O31-A1	**door-keeper**
iry-pat (rpa)	r:p:a	**hereditary nobleman**
irt	ir:tZ1	**eye**
irwy	ir:ir	**eyes, two eyes**
iri	ir:r	**to do, make, carry out, undertake, to spend (time),to act, serve, to beget, engender**
irw	i-ir-w-A53	**form**

irp	i-r:p-W22:Z2	**wine**
irf	i-r:f	**then, now**
irrtt	i-ir:t*t-W23:Z2	**milk**
irtyw	i-ir-tyw-A2-Z3	**mourning**
ihw	i-h-w-O1	**camp (military)**
ihm	i-h-m-D54	**to linger, lag, to be held back**
ihmt	i-h-G14-t:G37	**confinement**
ihhy	i-h:h-i-i-A28	**jubilation**
iH	i-H-E1	**ox, cow**
iH	i-H-O11	**palace**
iH	i-H-T24	**net, catch, snare**
iHw	i-H-w-O1	**stable (for horses)**
iHms	i-N41:z	**to sit down, reside, dwell, besiege**
ix	i-x:Y1	**please, then, so, therefore**
ixm-sk	i-x-m-D35-s-sk-k:N14	**indestructible** Lit. not knowing destruction
ixmt	i-x-m-t:N23*Z1	**river-bank, var: axmt**
ixr	i-x:r-A15	**Now..., Then..., Thus, Further**
ixxw	i-x:x-w-N8	**dusk, twilight, var. axxw**
ixt	i-x:t	**things**
is	i-s	**after all, indeed, even, in fact**
is	i-O35-D54	**go! Go, get...!**
is-HAq	i-O35-HA-q-D40:Z2	**easy prey, Lit. go and plunder**

is	i-M40-s-M2-Y1	**old, ancient, var. iswt**
iswt	i-M40-s-w:t-M2-Y1:Z2	**old times, antiquity**
is	i-M40-z:M2	**be light (in weight)**
is	i-M40-z:O1*Z1	**tomb, chamber**
isw	M40-s-Z7-A1	**look, behold**
isw	F44-w-Y1v	**exchange, payment**
isw	i-M40-s-w-F44:Y1	**exchange, payment**
isw	i-M40-s-Z7-M2:Z2	**reeds**
ist	M40-t:Z1	**crew (of ship), gang (of workers)**
istw	M40-Z7:t-A1-Z2	**crew (of ship), gang (of workers)**
iswt	i-M40-s-w:t-M2-Y1:Z2	**ancient times, antiquity**
is, isy	i-M40-z:M2	**to be light (of weight), frivilous, to be at ease**
ispt	i-s-p:t-M3	**quiver**
isft	i-s-f:t-G37	**injustice, wrongdoing, crime, falsehood, chaos**
isft	i-M40-s-f:t-G37	**evil, wrongdoing, isfty: sinner**
isr	i-z:r-M1:M3	**tamarisk**
isq	i-s-q-D56-D54	**linger, delay, restrain**
isk, sk	i-s-k, s-k	**Lo, Now,** enclitic particle
isT, ist	i-s-T, i-s-t	**Lo, Now,** enclitic particle
iSt	i-S:t-Y1:Z2	**property, belongings**
iSwt	i-S:t*Z9-Y1:Z2	**thing**
iSst	i-V6:z-t-A2	**What?**

iSd	i-Sd:d-M1	**type of tree**
iqr	i-q:r-Y1	**excellent, dependable, reliable, worthy, trusty; prosperous, wealthy**
iqr	i-q:r-Y1-A1	**worthy man**
iky	i-k-A19	**miner, hewer of stone**
iky	A19-i-i	**miner, hewer of stone**
ikb	i-k-D3	**mourn**
ikn	i-k:n-A24	**to draw water**
ikmw	i-km-m-Z7-F28	**shield**
ikn	i-k:n-A24	**scoop**
igrt	i-g:r:t	**however, moreover, now**
igrt	i-g:r-t:N25	**necropolis, thhe silent one**
it	U9:Z2	**barley**
it	i-t:f-A1	**father, my father**
itw	i-t:f-A1:Z2	**ancestors, fathers**
itw	i-t:f-Z7-G7-Z2:.	**ancestors, fathers**
ity	i-ti-i-i-G7	**sovereign**
ity	i-A2-ti-i-i-A23	**sovereign**
ity	I3:I3-G7	**soveriegn**
ity	I3:I3-A41	**sovereign**
itm, tm	t:tm-A40	**the sun god Atum**
itm	i-t:D38-A40	**the sun god Atum**
itmw	i-tm-m-Z7*G37:Z2	**suffocation, lack of breath**
itn	i-t:n-N5:Z1	**the sun, the solar disk**

	itn	i-t:n-A24	oppose, thwart
	itn	i-t:n-D19-A13	opponent, enemy
	itnw	i-t:n-D19-Y1:Z2	difficulties
	itnw	i-t:n-nw-w-D19-N33:Z2	ashes
	itrw	i-t:r-w-n:n:n	river, the Nile
	itrt	i-t:r:t-O20	row (of shrines, Upper Egypt)
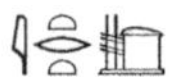	itrt	i-t:r:t-O19	row (of shrines, Lower Egypt)
	itH	i-t-H-A24	to draw, to drag up
	itH	i-t-H-V1:D40	drag, draw, stretch (a bow)
	itH	i-t-H-U31:O1	prison
	iTi	V15-A24	to take, take away, overcome, take possession
	iTA	i-TA-A-A24-A1	thief
	id	i-d:F21-Y1	sensless, deaf, dumb
	idt	N41:t-F45	vulva, cow
	idt	F45-t:N41	vulva, cow
	idt	D46A:t	fragrance
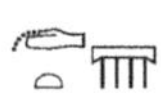	idt	D46A:t-N4	fragrance
	idyt	i-d-i-i-t-A17	girl, maid
	idw	i-d-w-N1	pestilence
	idw	i-d-w-N4	pestilence
	idb	N21:N23	river-bank, cultivated land
	idb	i-d-b-N21	river-bank, cultivated land

	**idbwy**	N21*N23:N21*N23	**the Two Banks (Egypt)**
	**idb**	i-d-b-N21	**the Two Banks (Egypt)**
	**idn**	i-d:n-F21:Y1	**replace**
	**idn**	F21:n-Y1v	**replace**
	**idnw**	F21:n-nw-w-Y1:A1	**deputy, substitute**
	**idr**	i-d:r-V37	**bind, bandage**
	**idr**	i-d:r-V37-E1	**herd, flock**
	**idr**	V37:Z1-E1	**herd, flock**
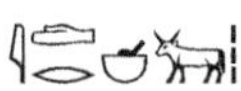	**idrw**	i-d:r-V37-E1-Z3	**herd, flock**
	**idHw**	i-d-H-w-M15	**the marshlands of te Delta**

idHy: Delta man

 y

	**y**	i-i	phonetic sound **y**
	**y**	y	Phonetic sound **y**
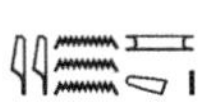	**ym**	i-i-n:n:n-N36:N21*Z1	**sea**
	**yH**	i-i-H-D54	**hey!**

 a

	a	a:Z1	arm, hand; condition, state
	a	a:W10	cup
	aw	a:S25	dragoman, interpreter
	aw	S25-w	dragoman, interpreter
	aw	S25-w-A2	dragoman, interpreter
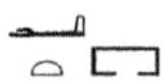	at	a:t-pr	room (of a building), department, house
	at	a:t*F51	limb (part of a body)
	aA	aA:a-M3	column
	aA	aA:a-A-Y1	great, large, grand
	aA	aA:a-A-Y1	greatness
	aA	aA:a-A-N31	here
	aA	aA:D52-E7	donkey
	aA	aA:O31	door,

iry-aA: doorkeeper

	aA-pr	aA:pr*pr	great-house, palace
	aAw	aA:a-A-w-Y1	great, greatly

aAt: greatly, greatness

	aAwt	aA:a-w-t*N33:Z2	lump
	aAppi	aA:p*p-I14	Apophis (giant serpent of the Dua
	aAm	T14-m-A1	Asiatic
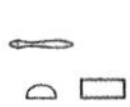	aAt	aA:t-O39	stone (valuable)

aAg	aA:A-g:a	to thrash, beat
aiai	a:a-i-A2	wail
aaft	a:a-f:t-Y1:Z2	rate of payment
aaw	a:a-w-S21	ring
aaw	a:a-w-D5	sleep
aab	a:a-b-F16:a	comb (hair)
aany	a:a-n:y-O1	tent
awAi	a:wA-A-a	to steal, to rob
awAi	a:wA-A-A24	rob, steal, robber, one robbed
awAw	a:wA-a:A1	robber
awA-ir.f	a:wA-A-a-ir:r:f	thief, brigand (he who steals)
awn	a-wn:n-A24	greedy, rapacious, defraud
awnt	a-wn:n-t:M3	stick, club
awt	T14-Z7:t-Z5:Z2	flock, sheep and goats
awt	S38-t-w-E8-Z3	flock, herd (small cattle), goats
awt	a-S38-w-t	awet-sceptre
ab	F16:Z1	horn, flank
ab	a-b-F16	horn
ab	a-b-F16:I3	horned crocodile
ab	a-b-F16:Y1	collect
ab	a-b-W10	cup, unite
abw	a-b-w-F17	purification

	**abA**	a-b-bA-A-S42	**aba-sceptre**
	**abA**	a-b-bA-S42-O39	**stela, table of offerings**
	**abA**	S42-Z1:O39	**stela, table of offerings**
	**aba**	a-b-a:F16-A2	**boasting, exaggeration**
	**abt**	a-b-t-O30	**fork**
	**api**	a:p*D54	**pass**
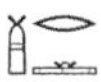	**apr**	Aa20-r:Y1	**to equip, provide, to have mastered**
	**afAy**	a:f-A-i-i-O1	**camp**
	**aff**	a:f:f-L3	**fly**
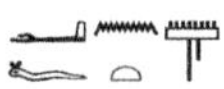	**afnt**	a:f-n:t-S28	**(royal) headress**
	**aft**	a:f:t-A36	**brewer**
	**afty**	A37-t:y	**brewer**
	**afdt**	a:f-d:t*pr	**box, chest**
	**afdt**	a:f-d:t*N23	**box, chest**
	**afdt**	a:f-d:t-M3	**box, chest**
	**am**	a-m-F10-A2	**to swallow, to devour**
	**ama**	a-m-a-A24	**smear**
	**amaAt**	a-m-a-A-t-T14	**throw-stick**
	**amam**	a-m-a-m-D51:D40	**to anoint, give a massage**
	**amat**	a-m-a:t-N23:Z2	**mud**
	**an**	a:n-D6:Y1	be **beautiful, pleasant**
	**an**	a:n-D8	be **beautiful, pleasant**

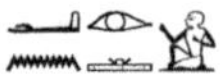	**an**	a:n-ir:Y1-A1	**the good man**
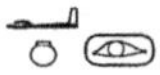	**anw**	a:nw-D8	**Anu, the limestone quarries at Turah**
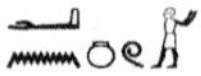	**anw**	a:n-nw-Z7-A31	**again**
	**ann**	a:n-n:D55	**to turn back, to go backwards, to face backwards, anw: one wo returns**
	**ann**	a:n:n-A31	**averted (face)**
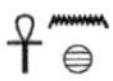	**anx**	anx-n:x	**to live, life**
	**anx**	anx-n:x-A2	**to swear, oath**
	**anx**	anx-Z1:V12	**garland**
	**anx**	anx-Z1:N34	**mirror**
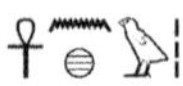	**anxw**	anx-n:x-w-Z3	**the living, ones who live**
	**anxw**	anx-Z1-N18:Z2	**victuals (food, provisions)**
	**anxt**	anx-n:x*t-U9:Z2	**grain**
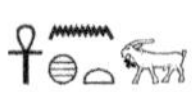	**anxt**	anx-n:x*t-E31	**goat**
	**anxtt**	anx-n:x:t*t-U9:Z2	**means of substance**
	**anxwy**	anx-anx-F21-F21	**ears, two ears**
	**anqt**	a:n-q:t	**the goddess of Anukis of Aswan**
	**ant**	a:n-t:D51	**finger-nail, claw**
	**anty**	G7A	**Anty (a god), 'He with Claws'**
	**anty**	G7B	**Anty (a god), 'He with Claws'**
	**antyw**	a:n-tyw-W23:Z2	**myrrh**
	**and, anD**	a:n-d:G37	be **few**

andt: a few (people)

	ar	a:r-N31	**ascend, penetrate**
	ar	a:r-M2	**reed (for writing)**
	arat	a:r-a:t-I12	**uraeus (protective serpent)**
	arryt	a:r:r-i-i-t:O1	**gate**
	arrt	a:r:r-t:O38	**gate, place of judgement**
	art	a:r:t-F19	**jaw**
	art	a:r-t-M2	**sheet (of papyrus or leather)**
	art	a:r:t-F22	**hind-quarters**
	arf	a:r-f-V6-D40	**sack, bag, envelop, tie up, bundle**
	arf	a:r:f-V6-A24	**sack, bag, envelop, tie up, bundle**
	arf	V33-A24	**sack, bag, envelop, tie up, bundle**
	arq	a:r:q-V12:Y1	**to be bent up, curved**
	arq	a:r:q-V12	**bind**
	arq	a:r:q-V12-A2	**understand**
	arq	a:r:q-V12:Y1	**wise, understanding**
	arq	a:r:q-V12	**wise, understanding**
	arq	a:r:q-V12-A2	**swear, take an oath**
	aqy	V12:q-i-i-N5	**last day of the month**
	aH	O11-a:O1	**palace**
	aH	a-H-T24	**net, catch, snare**
	aHAD	34-A-A24	**to fight, to wage war aHAwty: warrior**

Transliteration	Signs	Meaning
aHA	D34:D40	**to fight, to wage war**
aHA	aHA-A-T11:M3	**arrow weapon**
aHA	aHa-a:D54	**to stand up, to be standing, to rise, to attend**
aHa.n	aHa-a:n	introduces narrative past tense
aHaw	aHa-a:w-N5	**period, span of time, lifetime**
aHa	P6-a:P1	**boat (with mast)**
aHa	P6-a:D54	**stand up, go on duty, steadfast. arise**
aHa.n	P6-a:n	**then**
aHa	P6-a:M35-Y1:Z2	**heap, pile (riches), wealthy man**
aHa	P6-a:M35	**heap, pile (riches), wealthy man**
aHaw	P6-a:N5*Z1	**lifetime, period, space (of time)**
aHaw	P6-w-N5	**lifetime, period, space (of time)**
aHaw	P6-a-w-P1	**ships**
aHaw	P6-a:w-O26	**stela**
aHwty	T24-w-t*y:D40	**tenant farmer, field labourer**
aHwty	M2-Z7:t-y:D40	**tenant farmer, field labourer**
var: **iaHwty**	i-H-w-t*y:D40	**tenant farmer, field labourer**
aHt	T24-t:N21	**field, holding, domain**
ax	a:x-Q7	**brazier, fire (for cooking)**
ax	a:x	**brazier, fire (for cooking)**
axi	a:x-N1-A24	**hang up**

	**axm**	a:x-m-Q7	**quench, douse, extinguish (fire)**
	**axmt**	a:x-m-t:N23*Z1	**river-bank, var: axmt**
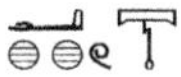	**axxw**	a:x*x-Z7-N2	**darkness, nightfall**
	**aXi**	a:X-H5	**to fly, fly off**
	**aXm**	a:X-m-G11	**divine image**
	**aXmw**	a:X-m-Z7-M2:Z2	**branches**
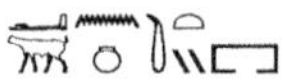	**aXnwty**	a:Xn-n:nw-ti-t:y-O1	**chamber, inner apartments**
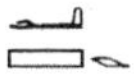	**aS**	a:S-M41	**pine (cedar of Lebanon)**
	**aS**	a:S-Aa2-A2	**groan**
	**aSA**	aSA-A-Z2:.	**many, numerous, rich**
	**aSAt**	aSA-A-t-A1:Z2	**multitude**
	**aq**	aq-q:D54	**to go in, enter**
	**aq-ib**	aq-q:D54-ib:Z1-A1	**intimate friend, confidant**
	**aqw**	aq-Z7-N18:Z2	**loaves, provisions, rations**
	**aqw**	a:q-w-U9:Z2	**loaves, provisions, rations**
	**aqA**	a:q-A-D50-D50-Y1	**straight, accurate, precise**
	**aqA**	a:q-A-D50-D50-Y1:Z2	**level, equality**
	**aqA**	a:q-A-D50-D50-Z7	**adjust**

aqAw: the right rope (in a ferry boat)

r-aqA: on a level with

s-aqA: put, set in order

	**atx**	a:t*x-A24	**to strain (a term used in beer making)**
	**ad**	a:d:Y1	**perceive, recognize**

Transliteration	Gardiner code	Meaning
ad	V26:d-Y1v	**be in good condition**
ad	V26:d-mr:D40	**hack up**
ad	V26:d-W22:Z2	**fat**
adw	V26:d-Z7-K3:Z1	**buri-fish**
adt	V26:d-t:P1	**the morning bark (ship) of the sun**

also: O.K. mnadt, mnaDt: the morning bark (ship) of the sun

Transliteration	Gardiner code	Meaning
aD	V26:Z1	**spool, reel**
aD	a:D-V26:M3	**spool, reel**
aD	V27:Z1	**spool, reel**
aD, aD	a:D-V26	**perceive, recognize**
aD	V26:d-Y1	**to be safe**
aD	a:D-V26:Y1	**be in good condition**
aD	aD:d-W22:Z2	**grease**
aD	aD:Y1	**to be safe**
aD	V26:D-N23:Z1	**desert-edge**
aDA	a-DA-A-D40	**guilty, guilt, crime**
aD-wDA	aD:Y1-w-DA-A-Y1	**to be safe and sound**
aD-mr	K3:N36	**administrator of a province lit. 'excavator of canals'**

, w

w	w-N21:Z1	**district**
w	w-N23:Z1	**district, region**
wA	wA-A-N31	**far, distant, long ago**
wAi	wA-N31	**fall, go off (into a state or condition)**
wAt	wA-A-t:V1	**coil of rope**
wAt	N31:t*Z1	**road, path, side, course**
wAt	wA-A-t-N31	**road, path, side, course**
wAw	wA-A-w-n:n:n	**wave (of ocean)**
wAwA	wA-A-wA-A-Y1:Z2	**interest (on loan)**
wAwA	wA-A-wA-A-A2	**ponder, deliberate**
wAwAt	wA-wA-t:V1	**coil of rope**
wAwAt	wA-wA-t:N25	**Wawat (North Nubian region)**
wAH	V29-H-Y1	**set, place, add, stop, remain, last, lasting**
wA-ib	V29-H-Y1-ib-Z1	**to be kind, patient, mercy, kindness, benevolent**
wAb	S40-b-S40-R12	**19th nome, Oxyrhchite U.E.**
wAH	wA-A-H-V29-Y1v	**place, put down, permit**
wAH	V29-H-Y1v	**place, put down, permit**
wAHyt	V29-H-i-i-t:M2	**increase, abundance of grain**
wAHw	wA-H-w-S10	**wreath**

wAxy V29-A-x:y-M15-O1 **columned hall, hall of the Inundation, reception hall in palace**

wAs	V4-A-s-S40-G37	**ruin**
wAs	S40-Z1	**was-sceptre**
wAs	S40	**dominion, lordship**
wAsi	wA-A-s-S40-G37	**be ruined, decay, ruin**
wAst	R19-t:O49	**Thebes (city of power)**
wAsty	R19-t*y:O49	**The Theban (an epiphet of Montu)**
wAS	wA-A-S-A28	**be exalted**
wAg	wA-A-g-A2	**to celebrate, make festival**

wAg wA-g:W3 **Wag-festival, celebrated on thhe 18th day of the first month (appearance of Orion)**

wAD	M13	**papyrus column**
wAD	wAD-A-D:Y1	**fresh, green, fortunate**
wAD	M14-Y1v	**success, good fortune**
wAD	M14-O39	**green stone, malachite**
wAdyt	M14-i-i-t-I13	**Wadjet-cobra goddess**
wAdt	M13-t-I13	**Wadjet-cobra goddess**
wADyt	M13-i-i-t:O1	**colonnade**
wAD-wr	M14-wr:r-N36	**the sea, the Great-Green**
wADb	wAD-b-F49:N23*Z1	**river bank**
wi	w-i-A53	**mummy case, mummy**

	**wi**	w-A1	**I, me**
	**win**	w-i-in:n-D40	**reject, put aside**
	**wiA**	w-i-A-P1	**sacred bark (boat)**
	**win**	w-i-in:n-D41	**reject, decline**
	**.wy**	w-y	dual ending
	**wa**	T21:a*Z1	**one, alone, individual**
	**wa**	wa:a*Z1-G37	**to be alone**
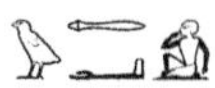	**waA**	w-aA:a-A2	**blaspheme**
	**waA**	w-aA:a-A-A2	**speak abuse**
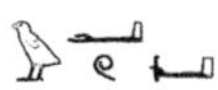	**waw**	w-a:Z7-D40	**soldier**
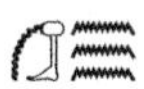	**wab**	D60-n:n:n	**pure, to purify oneself, to bathe oneself**
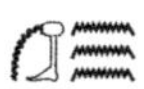	**wab**	wab-n:n:n	**purification**
	**wab**	wab-n:n:n-A1	**wab-priest**
	**wabw**	wab-n:n:n-w-F51:Z2	**meat offerings**
	**wabAyt**	U26-b-G29-A-i-i-t:Y1	**maid (servant)**
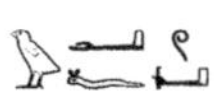	**waf**	w-a:f-V1:D40	**bend, curve**
	**war**	w-a:r-D56-D54	**fugitive**
	**wart**	Z7:a-r:t-D56-t:Z2	**flight**
	**wart**	w-a:r:t-D56	**leg, shank**
	**wart**	D56-t:N23	**district**
	**wart**	w-a:r-D56-t:N23	**administrative district**
	**wartw**	D56-t-w-A1	**district official**

waH	w-a-H-N11:N33*N33*N33	**carob-beans**
wbA	U26-b-bA-Y1v	**open up**
wbA	U26-b-bA-D6:O1	**open court**
wbA	U26-bA	**butler**
wbA	U26-nw-b	**butler**
wbAyt	U26-b-bA-A-i-i-t:Y1-B1	**maid**
wbn	w-b-n:N8	**to shine, rise (sun)**
wbnw	N8-nw*Z7:D26	**wound**
wbnw	w-b-n:nw*Z7-Aa2	**wound**
wbnw	N8-nw-w-F51	**wound**
wbd	w-b-d-Q7	to **burn**
wpi	F13:p*Z9	**to open, judge, divide**
wp-wAwt	wp:p-N31:Z2-A40	**Wepwawet (jackal god)**
wp-wAwt	E18	**Wepwawet (jackal god)**
wp-wAwt	wp:N31-t:Z2-E18	**Wepwawet (jackal god)**
wpw-Hr	wp:p-Z7:Z9-D2-Z1	**except, except for, apart from**
wpwt	wp:p-Z7:Z9-D2-Z1	**mission, business, message**
wpwtyw	wp:p-Z7-tyw-D54:Z2	**envoy, agent**
wpt	wp:t*Z1	**vertex, brow**
wpt	wp:p-t*Z9:V12	**land register**
wpt	wp:p*t-Z9-Y1:Z2	**specification**
wpt-rnpt	F14	**New Year's day**

wpt-rnpt F15 **New Year's day**

wpt-st Z9:Y1-s-t **specify it,** introducing list of items

wpt-tA wp:tA **Earth's Beginning (extreme south)**

wpt-tA wp:t*Z1-tA:N25 **Earth's Beginning (extreme south)**

wfA w-f-A-G39-A2 **talk, talk about, discuss**

wmwt w-D52:Z2-O1 **niche**

wmt w-D52:t:Y1 **thick**

wmt-ib: stout-hearted

wmt w-D52-Z3A-O1 **gateway**

wmtt w-D52-Z3A-O36 **fortification, bulwark**

wn wn:n-O31:D40 **to open**

wn wn:n-O31-A24 **to open**

wn-Hr **instructed, expert**

wn Hr n **light is given to (someone, that he may see), lit. face (ie sigt) is given to**

wn wn:n-G37 **failing, fault**

wni wn:n-D54 **pass by, disregard**

wnw wn:n-nw-w-O49 **Hermopolis, El-Asmunen, of U.E.**

wnwt wn:n-nw:t-N14:N5 **hour, time, moment, priestly duties**

wnwt N14:t*Z1 **hour, time, moment, priestly duties**

wnwt wn:n-t:sbA-A1:Z2 **hourly staff, priesthood**

wnwty wn:n-nw:t-sbA*N5:D4 **hour watcher, star watcher**

wnf wn:n-f-S28 **be glad, happy**

	**wnm**	wnm-m-A2	**to eat, consume**
	**wnm**	M42-m-A2	**to eat**
	**wnm**	wn:n-m-A2	**to eat**
	**wnmy**	R14-m-y:D41	**right hand**
	**wnmyt**	wnm-m-i-i-t-Q7	**the consumer, ie fire**
	**wnmw**	M42-A2-w-N18:Z2	**food**
	**wnmt**	M42-t-A2-X2*W22:N18-Z3	**food**
	**wnn**	wn:n:n	**to be, to exist**
	**wn-mAa**	wn:n-mA:Aa11	**reality, actual truth, true existence**
	**wn.in**	wn:n-i-n	**then**
	**wnn-nfr**	wn:n:n-nfr-f:r-A40	**Wenen-nefer, Osiris**
	**wnnt**	wn:n-n:t	**really, indeed**
	**wnx**	wn:n-x-V12:Z1	**to put on** (clothing)
		M42:N26-E1:Z2	**short horned cattle**
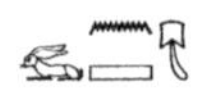	**wnS**	wn-n:S-F27	**jackal**
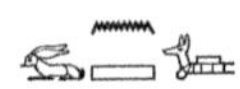	**wnS**	wn-n:S-U16	**sledge**
	**wnDw**	M42:N26-E3:Z2	**sort-horned cattle**
	**wnDwt**	M42:N25-t-w-A1*B1:Z2	**people, human beings**
	**wr**	wr:r	**great, much, very**
	**wr-n-if**	wr:r-n-i-f:F51	**haunch (of beef)**
	**wrr**	wr:r:r	**be great, important, much**

Word	Signs	Meaning
wr	wr:r-A20	**great one, ruler, prince**
wr-mAw	wr:r-mA:Z2-A1	**Greatest of Seers (high-priest of Heliopolis)**
wrt	wr:r:t	**greatness, very**
wrrt	wr:r-r:t-S2	**crown**
wrryt	wr:r-r-i-i-t-T17	**chariot, wagon**
wrrt	wr:r-r:t-M3	**chariot, wagon**
wrH	wr:r-H-W23:D40	**to anoint**
wrs	wr:r-s-Q4	**head-rest, pillow**
wrS	wr:r-S:N5	**spend the day, pass time**
wrSy	wr:r-S-i-i-N5-A1	**watchman**
wrd	wr:r-d-A7	**to be weary, tired**
wrdw	wr-d-Z7-A1-F34-Z1-B1	**the weary hearted**
whi	Z7-h-G37	**escape, miss, to fail, to be thwarted**
whn	w-h:n-O37-Z9:D40	**overthrow**
wHA	w-HA-A-A24	**pull up (papyrus, flax), hew (stones)**
wHAt	w-HA-t:Aa2-W10	**cauldron**
wHAt	Aa2:t-N34	**cauldron**
wHAt	w-H-HA-t*Aa2:N25	**Oasis region**
wHAt	Aa2:t-N25	**Oasis region**
wHAtyw	**Oasis dwellers**	
wHa	P4:a-V1:D40	**loose, break off work**
wHa	P4:a-V1-A2	**unravel, explain**

Transliteration	Gardiner codes	Meaning
wHa	P4:a-V1-A1	**fisherman, fowler**
wHyt	w-H-i-i-t-T14-A1:Z2	**tribe, tribesman**
wHwt	Z7-H-Z7:t-T14-A1*B1:Z2	**tribe**
wHyw	Z7-H-i-i-Z7-T14-A1*B1:Z2	**tribe**
wHm	F25-m	**repeat**
wHm	F25-m-Y1	**to repeat, to report**
wHm	F25-m-A2	**repeat**
wHmyt	wHm-m-i-i-t-A2	**howling**
wHmw	F25-m-Z7-A1	**herald**
wHmw	F25-m-A2-A1	**herald, provincial in charge of judicial matters**
wHmt	F25-t:Z1	**hoof**
wHt, Hwt	H-w-t:W6	**cauldron**
wx	w-x-R16	**fetish of the town Cusae U.E.**
wx	w-x-N2	**night**
wxt	w-x:t-N2	**night, darkness**
wxA	w-xA-M3	**(wooden) column**
wxA	w-xA-O1	**all of columns**
wxA	w-x-xA-A-G37-A2	**an incompetant person, a fool**
wxA	w-xA-A-G37-A1	**fool**
wxA	w-xA-A-G37	**be ignorant, fool**
wxA	w-xA-D54	**to fade** (colours)**, to empty out, purge**

	**wxA**	w-x-A-D54	**require, demand**
	**wxdw**	w-x:d-w-Aa2:Y1	**forebearance, tolerance**
	**wxd**	w-x:d-Aa2	**suffer, bear patiently, pain**
	**wsir**	ir:st-A40	**Osiris**
	**wsir**	Q2:D4	**Osiris**
	**wsir**	F51:r-A40	**Osiris**
	**wsf**	w-z:f-G39-D54	**be idle, idleness**
	**wsfw**	w-z:f-w-G41-D54-A1	**forgetter**
	**wsr**	F12-s-r:D40	**strong, powerfu, mighty, rich, wealthy**
	**wsr**	wsr-s-r:M3	**oar**
	**wsr**	wsr-s-r-P8	**oar**
	**wsrt**	wsr-t:Z1	**neck**
	**wsS**	w-z:S-D52	**urinate**
	**wsx**	w-s-x:W10	**cup**
	**S-n(y)-wsrt**	F12-s-r:t:n:n	**Senwosret**
	**wsx**	w-s-x*W10:Y1	**width, broad, wide**
	**wsxt**	W10*t:O1	**broad hall, judgement hall**
	**wsxt**	O15	**broad hall, judgement hall**
	**wsxt**	Z7-s-x:t*W10-P1	**barge (broad boat)**
	**wsTn**	w-s-T:n-D54	**to stride, to travel freely**
	**wS**	w-S:D3	**fall out (hair), be bald, free, unoccupied (of time)**
	**wSA**	w-SA-A-D51:D40	**fatten**

	**wSA**	Z7-SA-A-G41-A24	**fatten**
	**wSA**	w-S-G42	**fatten**
	**wSA**	G42	**fatten**
	**wSA**	w-SA-A-A2	**heap (praises)**
	**wSa**	w-S:a:F18	**chew, bite**
	**wSb**	w-S-b-Z9-A2	**to answer, reply, respond**
	**wSm**	w-S-m-H2-M2	**ear (of corn)**
	**wSmw**	H2-m-w-W22	**a vessel for beer**
	**wSn**	w-S:n-H4:a	**to wring the neck, sacrifice** (birds)
	**wSn**	w-S:n-G54	**wring neck (of birds), make offering of**
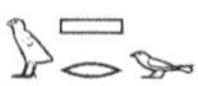	**wSr**	w-S:r-G37	**dry up, be barren**
	**wSd**	w-F30:d-A2	**address, question, respond to, speak to**
	**wgg**	w-g:g-G37	**dry up, be barren**
	**wgg**	w-V33-V33-G37	**dry up, be barren**
	**wt**	Aa2:D40	**to bandage, wrap mummy**
	**wt**	w-t:Aa2	**bandage, mummy wrappings**
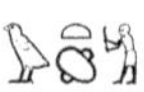	**wt**	w-t:Aa2-A24	**wrap mummy, to bandage**
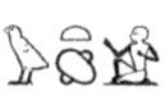	**wt**	w-t:Aa2-A1	**embalmer**
	**wtAw**	w-t:U30-A-Z7-S28-Z1:Z2	**bandage**
	**imy-wt**	i-imi-w-t*Aa2:O49	**he who is in the mummy wrappings,** an epiphet of Anubis
	**wtx**	w-t:x-D56-D54	**flee, wtxw: fugitive**

	**wtt**	w-t*t:D52	**beget**
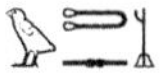	**wTs**	w-T:z-U39	**lift up, carry**
	**wTs**	w-T:z-U39-A2	**to make an accusation, denounnce**
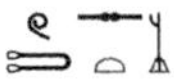	**wTst**	Z7:T-z:t-U39	**post (of balance)**
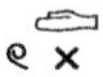	**wdi**	Z7-d:Z9	**to put, to plant, to carry off, carry out**
	**wdi**	w-d:D40	**put, push, shoot, inflict, emit (sound)**
	**wdpw**	W22-w-A1	**waiter**
	**wdb**	w-d-b-F46:a	**turn**
	**wds**	Z7-d-b-F46:D54	**to fold over**
	**wdf**	w-d:f-G39-D54	**to delay, to stall, be late**
	**wdn**	w-d:n-U32-O39	**to be heavy, oppressive, grevious**
	**wdn**	w-d:n-M11	**offer, make offerings**
	**wdn**	M11:n-Y1v	**offer, make offerings**
	**wdH**	w-d-H-W15	**pour**
	**wdHw**	w-d-H-w-R3	**table of offerings**
	**wdHw**	R3	**table of offerings**
	**wD**	w-wD-Y1\R270	**command, order**
	**wDwt**	wD-w-t:Y1	**command, order**
	**wD**	wD-w-O26	**stele, monumental inscription**
	**wD**	wD-w-V12	**stele, monumental inscription**
	**wDA**	w-DA-A-Y1	**sound, in good condition, prosperous, to be glad, happy**

Transliteration	Signs	Meaning
wDAt	w-DA-D10	**wedjat eye** (of Horus)
wDA	w-DA-A-D54	**to go, set out, proceed**
wDA	w-D:a-Aa21:Y1	**to judge, to cut** (cord), **to cut off** (head), **to be separated** (lips of a wound)
wDA	w-DA-A-O1	**magazine, storehouse**
wDAt	Aa21-t:Y1-B1	**divorced woman**
wDi	V25-w-D54	**send forth, set forth**
wDa	w-D:a-Aa21-Y1v	**divide, sever, judge**
wDat	w-D:a-Aa21-B1	**divorced woman**
wDyt	V25-i-i-t:D54	**(military) expedition**
wDww	wD-w-w-E1:Z2	**roaming cattle, wandering herds**
wDb	wD-b-N20:Z1	**river bank**
wDb	wD-b-F46:N21*Z1	**sand bank, shore**
wDb	V25-b-F46:D54	**turn**
wDbw	M13-b-w-M11:N21*Z2	**sand bank, shore**
wDnw	w-D:n-nw-w-N35A	**torrent, flood**
wDH	V25-H-A17	**child, weanling**
wDH	V25-H-A18	**princeling**
wDH	V25-H-nw:D40	**pour**
wDH	V25-H-Q7	**cast (metal objects)**
wDHw	V25-H-w-R3	**table of offerings**
wADb	wAD-b-F49:N23*Z1	**river bank**

b

Transliteration	Signs	Meaning
bA	R7-E10	**ram**
bA	bA-Z1	**the ba, soul**
bA	G53	**the ba, soul**
bA	bA-W10A-G7	**the ba, soul**
bA	R7-G29-Z1	**the ba, soul**
bAw	G30-Y1:Z2	**souls, might, power**
bA-pf	W10A-E10-p:f	**Bapfi, a god**
bAbA	b-bA-b-bA-N33	**hole, hiding place**
bAbAt	b-bA-A-b-bA-t-N35A	**flowing stream, swhirl**
bbt	b-b-t:N35A	**flowing stream, swhirl**
bAt	b-bA-A-t:M2	**shoot, wisp, ear** (of grain), **bush**
bAw	b-bA-Z7-P1	**galley** (boat propelled by oars)
bAH	b-bA-A-H-D53:F51	**foreskin**
bAH	b-bA-A-H-D53:Y1	**before, presence of**
bAH	D53:Y1	**before, presence of**
bAHi	D52:Y1-A50	**ancestor, predecessor**
bAXw	b-bA-A-X-w-N25	**Bakhu (Western Mountains)**
bAs	b-bA-s-W2	**jar**
bAstt	W2-t:t	**the cat-goddess Bastet**
bAstt	b-bA-A-Q1-t:Z5-I13	**Bastet** (goddess)

Hieroglyphs	Transliteration	Sign codes	Meaning
	**bAq**	bA-q-M1	**an oil bearing tree**
	**bAk**	bA-k:D40	**to work**
	**bAk**	bA-k-A24	**to work**
	**bAk**	bA-k:D40	**work, labour**
	**bAk**	bA-k:.-A1	**male servant**
	**bAkw**	bA-k:Y1:Z2	**tribute, work, produce**
	**bAkt**	bA-k:t-B1	**female sevant**
	**bAgi**	b-bA-A-g-A7	**be remiss, slack**
	**bAgi**	b-pA-A-g-A-i-i-A7-G37	**to be lazy, tired**
	**bAgi-ib**	b-pA-A-g-A-i-i-A7-G37-F34-Z1	**half-hearted**
	**bAgsw**	b-bA-A-g-sw-w-N34	**dagger**
	**bit**	bit-t:Z1	**bee**
	**bit**	L2-t-W23	**honey**
	**bit**	bit-t-W22:Z2	**honey**
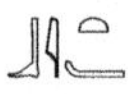	**bit**	b-i-t:F18	**character, qualities**
	**bit**	b-i-t-A2	**character, qualities**
	**bit**	b-i-W10:F18-t-A2	**character, qualities**
	**bity**	bit-t:y-A45	**king of Lower Egypt**
	**biA**	b-i-A-W10-Y1:Z2	**a marvel, miracle**
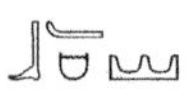	**biA**	b-F18:N41-N25	**heaven, firmament**
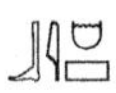	**biA**	b-i-N41:O39	**copper**
	**biA**	b-F18:N41-N1	**heavens, black material of the heavens**

biAw	b-F18:N41-w	**produce of mine**
biAw	b-F18:N41-w-N25:Z2	**mining region**
biAyt	b-F18:N41-i-i-t:N25	**heaven, firmament**
bia-n-pt	b-i-A-N21-F18:O39:Z2-n-p*t:N1	**iron** (meteoric), **metal-of-heaven**
biA-km	b-i-N41-O39-N41:I6	**black basalt**
bin	b-i-n:G37	**bad**
binr	b-i-n:r-M30-U9:Z2	**dates**
bint	b-n:t:M3	**harp**
bik	b-i-k-G6	**falcon**
baH	b-a-H-K2-A2	**to stink, reek**
baHi	b-a-H-G32-N35A	**be inundated, inundation**
baHi	G32	**be inundated, inundation**
bw	b-w	**thing, place, position**
bw	b-Z1	**thing, place, position**
bwAw	b-wA-w-A22-Z3	**magnates (great noblemen)**
bw-wr	b-w-wr:r	**the greater part**
bw-nb	b-Z7:nb-A1*B1:Z2	**everyone**
bw-nfr	b-Z7-nfr-f:r	**goodness**
bwt	b-w-t:K2	**abomination**
bw-Dw	b-Z7:N25-Z7-G37	**evil**
bw	b-Z7	late Egyptian negation: **not**

bw b:n late Egyptian negation: **not**

bnw b-n:nw*w-G31 **phoenix**

bnt b-n:t:M3 **harp**

bnt b-n:t-Y7 **harp**

bnwt b-n:nw-w-t-O39 **grindstone, millstone**

bnbnt b:n-b:n-t **pyramidion**

bnr b-n:r-i-M30-Y1 **sweet, pleasant**

bnrw b-n:r-w-O1 **outside**

bnS b-n:S-M3 **doorpost**

bhA b-h-A-D54 **flee**

bhAw: fugitive

bHs F18:z-E3 **calf**

bHs b-H-s-D56 **hunt**

bHs b-H-s-D40 **hunt**

bHs b-H-s-D54 **hunt**

bHdt F18:d-t:O49 **Behdet, Tell el-Balamun**

Town in northenmost Egypt

bxn b-x:n-O1 **tower, fortress**

bxnw b-x:n-nw-w-O39 **dark hard stone of Wady Hammamat, greywacke. Used in making cosmetic palettes etc**

bs b-s-K5:D54 **to introduce, to initiate**

bs b-s-K5:Y1 **mystery, mysterious form**

bsi b-s-K5:D54 **flow, come forth in abundance**

bSi	b-S:D26	**vomit**
bSt	b-S:t-D19	be **rebellious**
bkA	b-kA-B2	be **pregnant**
bgi	b-g-A7	**be remiss, slack**
bgAw	b-g-A-w-N35A-A1	**one shipwrecked**
bgs	b-g:z-G37	be **bad, fractious**
bgsw	b-g-sw-w-T8A	**dagger**
btA	b-t:U30-A-D56-D54	**run**
btA	b-t:U30-A-G37	**crime, wrong, wrong-doer**
bt	b-V15:t	**abandon, forsake**
btn	b-t:n-D19-A24	be **disobedient, rebel against**
bT	b-V15	**abandon, forsake**
bTn	b-T:n-D19	be **disobedient, rebel against**

bTn-ib: rebel, adversary

bd	b-d-R9	**a kind of natron**
bdt	R9	**a kind of natron**
bdt	M34-d:t-U9:Z2	**emmer** (wheat)
bdt	b-d:t-M34	**emmer** (wheat)
bdt	b-d:t-U9	**emmer** (wheat)
bdty	M34-t:y-M33	**emmer** (wheat)
bdS	b-d:S-A7	**weary, to become faint, weak**

p

▯ p

p	p	phonetic sound '**p**'
p	p:N37	**base, pedestal**
p	p:O49	**Pe, Kom Farain, Buto, town in L.E.**
pt	p*t:N1	**sky, heavens**
pA	G40-A	**the, this**
pAy.i	pA-i-i-A1	**my**
pA	p-G41-A	**to have done in the past, used to**
pA	p-pA-A-H5	**fly**
pAwt	pA-A-w:t-Z8:Z2	**offering loaves**
pAwt	pA-A-w-t-X6:Z8	**offering loaves**
pAwt	X6:t	**primeaval time, antiquity**
pAwt-tA	X6:t-N18	**primeaval time of the earth**
pAq	p-pA-A-q:H3	**a kind of cake**
pAqt	H2-q:t-S28	**fine linen**
pAqt	H2-q:t*Z5-S28-Z3	**fine linen**
pqt	p:q-t-H2-V12:W23	**fine linen**
pAqyt	G41-A-q-i-i-t:O39	**sherd**
pAtpA-t:X6		**loaf, bread-offering**
pAtpA-t:X6		**antiquity, primeval times**
pAdpA-A-d-D56-F51		**knee**
pAD	pA-A-D:S21	**ball**

pis	p-i-s-A24	**bring in corn (on back of donkeys)**
pat	p:a-t:X6	**loaf of bread**
pat	p:a:t-A1*B1:Z2	**the elite, mankind, patricians**
pat	p:a-t:H8-A1*B1:Z2	**the elite, mankind, patricians**
piw	p-i-w-F27-Z3	**fleas**
pw	p-w	**It is.../They are..., this, who? what? whichever?**
pwtr	p-w-t:r-M4-A2	**Who...? What...?**
ptr	p*t:r-M4-A2	**Who...? What...?**
pty	p:t*y-M4-A2	**Who...? What...?**
pwy	p-w-i-	**this, that**
pwnt	p-wn:n-t:N25	**Punt**
pf	p:f	**that**
pfs	p:f:z-Q7	**cook, boil**
pn	p:n	**this, that**
pna	p:n:a-P1A	**overturn, upset**
pnw	p:n-nw-w-F27	**mouse**
pnq	p:n-q-A24	**bale out**
pr	pr:Z1	**house, household, temple, palace**
prw	pr:r-Y1:Z2	**excess**
pr-nsw	sw-t:n-O1:Z1	**palace, house of the king**
pri	p:r-i-M6-N21:Z1	**battlefield**
pr-aA	aA:pr	**great-house, palace, pharaoh**

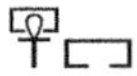	**pr-anx**	O54-O1	**House of Life (where books were written)**
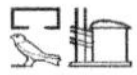	**pr-wr**	pr:wr-O19	**shrine at Hieraconpolis U.E.**
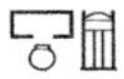	**pr-nw**pr:nw-O20		**shrine at Buto L.E.**
	**pr-nsr**	pr:Z1-n:ns-z:r-O20	**shrine at Buto L.E.**
	**pr-HD**	pr-T3-pr	**treasury, white (silver) house**
	**pr-HD**	O2	**treasury, white (silver) house**
	**prt**	pr:r-t:N5	**winter (growing** season)
	**prt**	pr:r-t:N33	**seed**
	**prt**	pr-r:t*Z5-U9:Z2	**seed**
	**pri**	pr:D54	**to go, come out, to ascend, go up**
	**pr-Djt**	pr:Z1-D:t:N17	**estate**
	**prt-xrw**	O3	**invocationn offerings**
	**pry**	pr:r-i-i-D54-E1	**champion, hero**
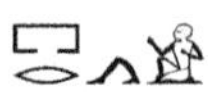	**pry**	pr:r-D54-A1	**champion**
	**pH**	F22:D54	**to reach, attain, attack, end up**
	**pH**	p-H-F22	**to reach, attain, attack, end up**
	**pHwy**	pH-w-y	**end, bottom, hind quarters**
	**pHwy-r**	pH-w-y-r	**down to**
	**pHwyt**	pH-w-y-i-i-t:V1	**stern-rope**
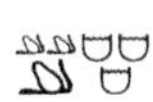	**pHww**	pH*pH:F22-N41*N41:N41	**distant marshlands**
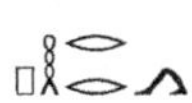	**pHrr**	p-H-r:r-D54	**run**
	**pHty**	pH-t*y:a	**might, power, strength**

pHt F9-F9 **might, power, strength**

pxA p:x-xA-A-V11:Y1 **split, break open**

pXr p:X-r-F46 **to circulate, to travel around, to pervade**

pXr p:X-r:D54 **turn, go round, serve**

pXr-wr F46:r-wr:r-n:n:n:N36 **Euphrates river**

pXrt F46:r-t-N33:Z2 **remedy, prescription** (medical)

pXrt F46:r-t-A24-A1:Z2 **frontier guards**

pXr-wr F46:r-N36 **river Euphrates**

psi p:f:z-Q7 **cook, boil, derived from**

older form: **fsi** f-s-Q7

psSt p:z-S:t*Z9-Y1:Z2 **portion, share, division**

psH p:z-H-F18-A2 **bite**

psx p:z-x:D54 **be in disorder, distraught**

psS p:z-S:Z9-Y1v **divide; psSw: divider (of property); psSt: division, share**

psg p:z-g-D26 **spit, spit upon**

psd, psD p:z-d:F37 **back**

psd p:z-d-F38 **back**

psd p:z-d-F39 **back**

psd p:z-d-F41 **back**

psDt N9:t-R8-R8-R8 **ennead, nine-gods**

psd, psD p:z-d:N5 **shine**

psDntyw N9:n:W3 **the new moon, the new moon festival**

psDntyw	N9:n-tyw-W3	**New-moon festival**
psDn	N9:n-W3	**New-moon festival**
psdn	p:z:d-n:N9	**New-moon festival**
pqw	p:q-w-N33	**a kind of cake**
pqt	p:q-t-S28	**fine linen**
pgA	p:g-A-D32	**spread out, unfold**
pgA	p:g-A-N23:Z1	**opening**
pty	p:t*y-M4-A2	**who? what?**
ptpt	p:t-p:t-D54	**trample, crush**
ptn	p:t-n:N25	**Peten** (a place name)
ptr	p*t:r-M6-A2	**who? what?**
ptr	p*t:r-M6-D5	**behold, see**
ptH	p:t-H-A40	**Ptah, god of Memphis**
pwtr	p-w-t:r-M4-A2	**Who...? What...?**
ptx	p:t-x:D54	**to cast to the ground, overthrow**
pd	p:d-D56-F51	**knee**
pd, pD	p:d-T9:D54	**stetch, be wide**
pd	T9:D54	**stetch, be wide**
pD	p:d-D56-D54	**to kneel, to run**
pds	p:d-s-D56-M3	**box, chest**
pdswt	p:d-s-w-t-D56-N21:Z2	**dunes (of the Delta coast)**
pDt	T9:t*Z1	**bow, foreign people, troop**

p

 **pDt** T9:t*Z1:M3 **bow, foreign people, troop**

 **pDt, pdt** p:d-t:T9-T14-A1 **bowman**

 **pDty** T14-A1 **bowman, foreigner**

 **pDt** T10:Z1*Z1*Z1*Z1*Z1*Z1:Z2 **the Nine Bows, the surrounding peoples and enemies of Egypt**

f

Transliteration	Signs	Meaning
f	f	phonetic **f**
.f	f	**he, him, his, it, its**
ft	f	**viper**
.fy	f:y	**dual ending**
fAi	f-A-A9-D40	**to raise, lift up, carry**
fAi-TAw	f-A-A9-D40-P5-w	**to sail before the wind, the wind picks up, accrue**
fAw	f:F40-w-Y1:Z2	**magnificance, splendour**
fAk	f-A-k:D3	**be bald, bare**
fn	f:n-G37	**be weak**
fnd	f:n-d-D19-Z1	**nose**
fnd, fnD	D19:Z1	**nose**
fnxw	f:n:x-w-V12:Z2	**Fenekhu (Syrians)**
fk	f:k-D3:G37	**be bald, bare**
fx	f:x-V12	**to loosen, to displace, to destroy, to fall to ruins, to obliterate, unloose, take off (garments), to depart**
fxy	f:x-V12-y:D54	**to loosen, to displace, to destroy, to fall to ruins, to obliterate, unloose, take off (garments), to depart**
fqA	f:q-A-X4:Y1	**to reward, wealth**
ft	f:t	**viper**
ftft	f:t-f:t-D54	**leap**
ftt	f:t*t-F37	**fibres, lint**

	**fd**	f:d-Z9:D40	**to pluck**
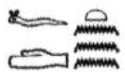	**fdt**	f:d-t:N35A	**sweat**
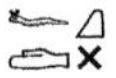	**fdq**	f:d-q:Z9	**tear asunder, piece, fraction**

m

Transliteration	Code	Meaning
m	m	phonetic sound **m**
m	m	**don't, do not**
m	m:a	**who?**
m	m:D38	**who?**
m	m:a	**take**
mi	m:D38	**now, please**
m	m	**in, inside, by means of, with, from, out of, into, being, namely, as, with, in the position of, being made of**
mA	mA:Z1	**sickle shaped end of a sacred boat**
im	i-m	**thereby,there, therewith, therein**
imy	i-imi-m-y	**who/which is in**
m-n.k	T1:n:k	**take**
m-a	m-a	**in the hand, in the posession of, by the hand of, with, because of, from the hand of, to happen to**
mm	m-m	**among** (people)
mm	m:a-m:a	**among** (people)
mt	m:a-t-n:n:n	**urine**
mAwy	mA-A-w-y-Y1v	**be new, fresh, new**
mAw	mA-A-Y1v	**be new, fresh, new**
mAwt	G3-Aw-w-t:N8-Z3	**rays**
mAt	mA:t-M1	**charm**
mAA	mA:Ir-A-A	**to see, to look at, to regard**

mAi mA-A-i-E22 **lion**

mAa mA:Aa11-a:H2 **side of the head, temple, to pay attention**

mAa mA:Aa11-a:Y1 **true, right, just, fair, correct, innocent**

mAa mA:Aa11-a:Y1 **guide, direct**

mAa mA:Aa11-a-H2:Y1 **true, right, just, fair, correct, innocent**

mAa U5:a-Y1v **be offered (offerings)**

mAaw: offerings, tribute

mAa U5:a-H2 **temple (of head)**

mAa U5:a-N21:Z1 **edge, brink**

mAa Aa11:D54 **send, dispatch**

mAa-xrw U4:a-xrw-w-A2 **True-of-Voice, jutstified, vindicated**

mAa-xrw Aa11\R270-P8 **True-of-Voice, jutstified, vindicated**

mAaw mA:Aa11-a-w-H2-P5 **proper wind**

mAat U4:a-t-H6-Y1:Z2 **truth, justice, order**

MAat U4:a-t-C10 **Maat** (goddess of Truth)

mAw mA-A-w-Y1 **new**

mAwt mA-A-w-t:Y1 **something new, a new thing**

mAr, mAi mA-A-i-r:T12-G37-A2 **poor**

mAar mA:ir-A-r:T12-G37 **wretched**

	**mAH**	mA-A-H-M2	**wreath (of flowers)**
	**mAHD**	mA-HD-E28	**oryx**
	**mAX**	mA-A-X-Q7	**smolder, burn, be consumed**
	**mAst**	A-st-t-D56	**lap, thighs**
	**mAgsw**	mA-g-sw-w-N34	**dagger**
	**mAT**	mA:T-W7	**red granite (from Elephantine)**
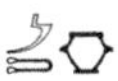	**mAT**	mA:T-W7	**proclaim**
	**mi**	m-i-D54	**come**
	**mi**	mi-i	**like**

mi qd.f: entire; mi m: how?

	**mi-m**	mi-i-m:a	**how 'like what'**
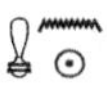	**min**	mi-n:N5	**today**
	**minA**	mi-i-n-A	**here, like this**
	**mini**	mn:n-i-T14-A14	**moor, 'die'**
	**mit**	mi-t	one **which is equal, one like** it**, copy, likeness**
	**mitw**	mi-t-w-A1	**one's equal, like**
	**mitn, miTn**	m:a-t:n-G41-N31	**path**
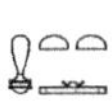	**mitt**	mi-t*t:Y1	**likeness, a thing like**
	**mitt-iry**	mi-t*t:Y1-i-r:y	**something like it**
	**mi**	m:a-i-y:D54	**come!**
	**mar**	m-a:r-M30-Y1	**successful, fortunate**
	**maHat**	m-P6-a:t*M35	**cenotaph, funerary monument**

makA m-a:k-A-A24 **brave**

mk m-a:k **Look**

mw n:n:n **water**

mwt G14-t-B1 **mother**

mwt m-t:Z6 **die**

mwt-nsw sw-mwt **Mother of the King**

mwt-mwt mwt-G14-t **grandmother**

mbi m-b-i-A2 **umbii** (sound of a baby), **No!**

m-biA m-b-i-A-W10:F18-Y1:Z2-A2 **No!**

mfkAt m-f:D28-t:N33:N33:N33 **turquoise** (stone)

mm m-m-a **among**

mmy m:a-m:a-F27 **giraffe**

mn mn:n:Y1 **to endure, to be enduring, to be firm, to remain**

mn mn:n-Y1:A1 **such a one**

mnt mn:n-Y1:B1 **such a one**

mnt mn:n:Y1 **such an amount**

mnw mn:nw*nw*nw **monuments**

mn-nfr mn:n-nfr-f:r-O24-O49 **Men-nefer, Memphis**

mn-xpr-ra <-N5-mn:n-xpr-> **Men-kheper-ra** (Thutmose III)

mn mn:n-G37 **to be sick, suffer, to suffer from**

mn mn:n-G37:Y1-A1 **sick man, pain**

mniw A33-Z7:Y1 herder

mnw R22:R12 Min (god)

mnt mn:n-t-G37:Z2 sickness, illness, pain

mnt mn:n-t:N5 m mnt: daily

mnt mn:n-t:G36 swallow (bird)

mnt mn:n:t-D56 thigh

mni mn:n-i-T14-P1 to moor (ship), to bring to port,

to bring one's venture to port

mni mn:n-i-P11-A24 moor, land, attach, join

mni mn:n-i-T14-P1 moor, land, attach, join

mnit mn:n-i-t-P11-M3 mooring post

mnit mn:n-i-t-S18 necklace with counterpoise

mni mn:n-i-Z9:W22 a measure for oil or incense

mna mn:n-a:D27-B5 nurse, suckle

mnat: nurse, foster-mother; mnay: tutor

mniw A47-w herdsman

mniw mn:n-i-w-A33 herdsman

mniw A33 herdsman

mnyt mn:n:f-i-i-t-A12-Z3 soldiers

mnw mn:nw*nw*nw monuments

mnw R22:R12-C8 Min,

god of Panopolis (Akhmim) and Coptos (Kift)

mnw mn:nw*nw*nw-M1-M1-M1 **trees**

mnwt mn:nw*t-G39 **pigeon**

mnmn mn:n-mn:n-D54 **to quake, shake** (of earth)

mnmnt mn:n-mn:n-t-E1:Z2 **cattle**

mnnw mn:n:n-nw-w-O1 **fortress**

mnw mn:n:nw-O1 **fortress**

mnhd, mnhD mn:n-h:d-Y3 **writing outfit**

mnH mn:n-H-N33:Z2 **wax**

mnH mn:n-H-M2 **papyrus plant**

mnx mn:n-x-U22 **fashion, carve, a chisel**

mnx mn:n-x-U22:Y1 **beneficient, potent** (of king), **dependable, trusty** (of officials), **excellent, be efficient**

mnx mn:n-x-U22-V1 **string (of beads), fasten (amulet on neck)**

mnxt mn:n-x:t-S27 **clothing**

mnxt S27 **clothing**

mnS mn:n-S:V10 **cartouche**

mnqb mn:n-q-b-W15 **bed-chamber**

mnTw mn:n-T-w-A40 **Montu** (god of war), the falcon headed god of Hermonthis (Armant)

mnTw mn:n:T-w-T14-A1:Z2 **Beduins of Asia**

mnd mn:n-d:D27 **breast**

mnDm mn:n-nDm-V19 **basket, crate**

imy-r m:r **overseer**

imy-r m-r:. overseer

imy-r F20 overseer

mr N36:N21*Z1 canal

mr U23-m:r-G37 sick, painful, pain, ailment

mr U23-m-r:G37-A1 sick man

mrwt U23-m-r:t-G37:Z2 pains

mrwt m gs tp U23-m-r:t-G37:Z2-m-gs:Z1-tp:Z1 **migraine head ache pains,** Lit: **pains in side of head**

mr U23-m:r-O24-O1 **pyramid**

mr mr:r-A2 **to love, like**

mr U7:r-V1:D40 **bind**

mr N36:N23-A1-B1-Z3 **friend(s), partisans**

HAw-mr: **the multitudes, the masses** HA-A-w-Y1:Z2-N36-A1*B1:

mri mr:r-A2 to **desire, want, like, love, wish**

mri mr-r:N36 to **love, wish**

mri U7:r-i-M6-O49 **mri** in the name:

Ta-meri A-U7:r-i-M6-O49 **Egypt (Land Beloved)**

Mry mr:r-i-i-A1 **Mery** (man's name)

mryn m-a-r:Z1-i-i-n:A-T14-A1 **Syrian noble, mariannu**

mryt mr:r-i-i-t:N23*Z1 **shore, bank, quay**

mryt mr:r-i-i-t-B1 **Meryt** (woman's name)

mrw U7:r-w-N25 **desert**

mrw	U7:r-w-M41-M3	**a red wood from Syria**
mr-wr	U7:r-wr:O5-E1	**Mnevis, sacred bull of Heliopolis**
mr-wr	O5-wr-E1	**Mnevis, sacred bull of Heliopolis**
mrrt	mr-r:r-t:O5-O1	**street**
mrrt	U7:r-r:t-O38	**street**
mrt	N36-A1-B1-Z3	**weavers**
mrt	N36:N21*Z1-A1*B1:Z2	**weavers**
mrt	U7:r:t-A1*B1:Z2	**slaves, serfs**
mrt	mr-r:t-A2-B1	**Merit** (woman's name)
mrt	mr:r-t:D6-G7	**Meret (goddess of song)**
mryt	mr:r-i-i-t:N23*Z1	**river bank**
mrwt	mr:r:t-A1*B1:Z2	**serfs, dependents**
mrw	mr:r-Z7	**Meru** (man's name)
mrwt	mr:r-w-t-A2	**love, wish, for the sake of**
n-mrwt	n-mr:r-w-t-A2	**in order that**
mrryt	mr:r-r-i-i-t-N18:Z2	**lumps of insence?**
mrH	U7:r-H-G37	**decay**
mrHt	mr:r-H-t-W23:Z2	**oil, fat, ointment**
mrHt	U7:r-H-t-W1	**ungent oil**
mrHt	W1	**ungent oil**
mhy	m-D38-h:y-G37	**be forgetful, negligent**
mhi	m:D38-h-A-G37-F34-Z1	**to be forgetful, to forget**

mwt G20-h-w-t-A1*B1:Z2 **family, household**

mhr m:a-h:r-W19 **milk-jug**

mH V22:Y1 **to fill, to be full**

mH V22:D40 **to seize, grasp, take**

mH V22:D42 **cubit** measure of length 52.3 cm

mH V22 participle for **ordinal numbers** 10 and higher

mHy V22:a-i-i-A2 **to feel sorry**

mH mH:a-A2 **be anxious, grieve, care**

mHy mH:a-H-y:F37B-A2 **be anxious, grieve, care**

mHy mH:a-H-y:F37B-M2:Z2 **flax**

mH mH-H-N35A **drown**

mHw mH-H-w-M15 **papyrus clump**

Ta-mHw: tA:mH-H-w-M15 **The Delta L.E., 'Land of Papyrus'**

mHw mH-w-P1:K5-A1 **fish-spearer**

mHyt mH-H-i-i-t-K5:Z2 **fishes**

mnHyt mH:n-i-i-t-I12 **uraeus, the Coiling one on the head of sun-god and king**

mHyt mH-H-i-i-t-P5 **northwind**

mHt mH:t-W22 **dish**

mHt mH:t **north**

mHt mH:t*N21*Z1 **north**

mHty V22:t*y **northern**

mHtyw	V22:t:Z2	**northerners**
mHty-int	V22:t*y-R14-t*N21:Z2	**north-west**
mxA	m:a-xA-A-D50-D50-Y1v	**to balance, equal**
mxAt	m:a-xA-A-t-U38	**balance, scales**
mxAt	m:a-xA-A-t-U39-M3	**balance, scales**
mxmt	m-x:t-m-t:S20-O32	**sealed chest**
m-xt	m-M3:x*t-D54	**accompanying, after, when**
mXnt	m:a-Xn:n-t:P1	**ferry-boat**

mXnty: ferryman

mXr	m:a-Xr:r-O1	**barn, storehouse**
mXr	m:a-Xr:r-N23:Z1	**low lying land**
mXr	m-a:Xr-r:O1	**storehouse**
mXrw	m-a-Xr:r-w-Z2:.	**affairs, dealings, business**
mXrw	m:a-Xr:r-w-Y1:Z2	**administration, governance**
ms	m-D38:O35	**to transport, to deliver**
ms	m:a-O35-D54	**bring**
ms	m-O35	**bring**
ms	ms-s-A2	**indeed, surely, truly**
ms	ms-s-B3	**to give birth, bear a child, fashion statues**
msi	ms-s-B3	**bear, give birth, form, fashion**
msw	ms-s-w-A1*B1:Z2	**offspring, children**
msyt	ms-s-i-i-t-N18:Z2	**supper**

Transliteration	Code	Meaning
msyt	ms-s-i-i-t-N2-N18:Z2	**supper, evening meal**
msyt	ms-s-i-i-t-G41:Z2	**water fowl**
msn	V32:O49	**Mesen, a town near Kantarah in Lower Egypt**
msnw	ms-n:nw*Z7-V32-A1	**harpooner, hippopotamus-hunter**
msnH	ms-s-n-H-D55	**to turn backwards, to rotate around**
msH	m-s-H-I3	**crocodile**
msxn	ms-s-x:n-O1	**resting-place**
msxtyw	ms-x-tyw-U19	**adze**
msxtyw	ms-s-x-tyw-F23:N14-A40	**the Foreleg, the constellation of the Great Bear**
mss	ms-s-s-N34	**corslet**
mss	ms-s-s-F27	**corslet**
mskA	ms-s-kA-F27	**hide (of ox)**
mski	ms-s-k-i-A2	**gossip, rumour**
mst	F31-t	**apron of fox skins**
mstywty	ms-s-tyw-t:y	**descendant (of a god)**
mstpt	ms-s-t:p-t:M3	**bier (at funeral)**
msTpt	ms-T:p*t-O18	**portable shrine**
mstpt	ms-s-t:p-M3	**portable shrine**
msd, msD	ms-s-d-A2	**to hate, dislike**
msdw	ms-s-d-w-A2	**rival, adversary**
msdmt	ms-s-d-m-t-N33:Z2	**eye paint (black)**

msDi	ms-s-D-A2	**hate**
msDr	ms-s-Dr:r-F21	**ear**
mSa	m-S:a-A12	**army**
mSa	A12-A1:Z2	**soldiers, troops, army, gang, crew**
mSa	A12-P1	**military expedition**
mSrw	m:a-S:r-E23-Z7-N2	**evening**
mSdt	G20-Sd:d-t:N21*Z1	**ford**
mk	m-D38:k	**look, see**
mk	m-D42:k	**look, see**
mk	m:D42-k:.	**look, see**
makA	m-D42:k-A-D42	**brave**
mki	m-a:k-A24	**protect**
mkwt	m-a:k-t:Y1:Z2	**protection**
mkHA	m-D38:k-HA-D1	**neglect**
mkty	m-a:k-t:y-A24	**protector**
mkt	m-a:k-t:Y1	**right place**
mkti	m-D38:k-ti-i-N25	**Megiddo** (a town in Canaan)
mgA	Aa15:a-g-A-A17	**a class of young recruits**
mt	m-D38:t	**behold! (in addressing a female)**
mt	D52:t*Z5	**vessel (of the body), vein, muscle**
mt	m-t-A14	**to die, to perish, death**
mt	m-t-Z6	**to die, to perish, death**

mty	D52:t-D50-D50-Y1	**exact, correct, faithful, loyal, straightforward, regular, trustworthy**
mty	D52:t*y-T14-T14-Y1	**exact, correct, faithful, loyal, straightforward**
mty	D52:t-y-A1	**controller**
mty-n-sA	D52:t*y-A1:n-V17-A1:Z2	**controller of (priestly) phyle**
mtwt	D52:t-w-t-D53	**seed, poison**
mtwn, mTwn	D52:t-wn:n-E1-N23:Z1	**place of cobat for bulls**
mtr	D52:t:r-D50-D50-A2	**testify, bear witness, straightforward, advice**
mti	D52:t-D50-D50-Y1	**testify, bear witness, straightforward, advice**
mtr	D52:t:r-D50-D50-A2	**bear witness to**
mtrw	D52:t:r-w-T14-T14-A2-A1:Z2	**witnesses**
mtrt	D52:t-r:t-N5	**midday**
mT	m-D38:T	**look, see** (feminine)
mt	m-D38:t	**look, see** (feminine)
mTA	m-TA-A-A2	**taunt, flout, insult**
mTAm	m-TA-A-m-S28	**clinging dress for girls**
mTn	m-D38-T:n	**look, see** (plural)**, behold**
mtn	m-D38:t-n:Z2	**look, see** (plural)**, behold**
mtn	D52:t:n	**to reward**
mtnwt	D52:t:n-w-t-Y1v	a **reward**
mtpnt	m-t:p-n:t	**dagger T8 of the form**

	mTn, mtn	m-a:T:n-N31	**road**
	mtn, mwtn	mwt-t:n-N31	**road**
	mtn	m-a:t:n-T14-G41-A1	**nomad**
	mTn	m-D38:T-n:N25	**Mitanni, kingdom E. of Euphrates**
	mdw	md-d-w-A2	**to speak, talk**
	mds	m-d:z-T30:D40	**keen, alert**
	mdt	md-d:t-A2	**to speak, speech, words, thing, matter**
	mdw	md-Z1:M3	**staff, rod**
	mdw-iAwt	md-A19	**staff of old age**
	mdw-nTr	nTr-md	**hieroglyphs, divine words**

Dd-mdw: D-md **words to be recited**

	mD	V21-Y1v	**be deep**

mDwt: depth

	mDt	V21-t:O1	**stable, cattle-stall**
	mDt	m-D:t-V19	**stable, cattle-stall**
	mDt	m-D:t-W1	**ointment**
	mDAt	Y1:t*Z1-V12:Z1	**papyrus scroll, book**
	mDAt	Y1:t*Z1-N34	**scultor's chisel**
	mDAyw	m:a-DA-A-i-i-T14-A1:Z2	**Medjay, a Nubian people, police**
	mDw	V20	**ten**
	mDH	S10	**fillet**
	mDH	S10-H	**fillet**

 **mDH** S10-H-T30:D40 **to hew**

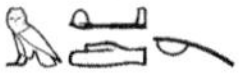 **mdH** m-D38:d-T7 **to hew**

 **mDH** T7-H-A24 **to hew, to build**

mDHw: carpenter

 **mDd** m-D38-D:d-Aa23-D40 **hit a mark, adhere to (a path)**

n

n	n	phonetic sound **n**
n	D35	**not, no**
n	n	**for, to, because of, belonging to**
ny	n:y	**therefore, for**
nw	n:Z2	**us, we**
nA	n:A	**these, the**
nAw	n:Aw-E30	**ibex**
nA-n	n:A-n	**these, the**
ni	n:i-D41	**reject**
niw	D41:Z1*W10	**bowl**
niw	n:i*w-D41-W22	**bowl**
niw	D41:n-w-G34	**ostrich**
niw	D41:Z7-G39	**ostrich**
niw, nw	nw:Z1	**therefor, for**
nis	n-i-s-A2	**summon, call, invoke**
nis	n:i*s-A26	**summon, call, invoke**
nitit	n-i-t-i-t-A2	**stammer**
naa	n:a:a-Y3	**be smooth**

snaa: polish, grind, fine

	**nai**	n:a-P1	**sail, travel by boat**
	ny	n	**of, belonging to**
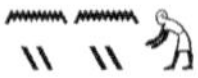	**nyny**	n:y-n:y-A16	**do homage**
	**ny-sw**	n:F20-sw-w	**he belongs to**
	**ny-sy**	n:F20-s-y	**she belongs to**
	**nw**	nw:Z1	**of**
	**nw**	nw	**of**
	**nwy**	n-w-y	**of**
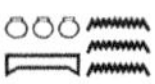	**nww, niw, nwnw**	nw*nw*nw:N1-N35A	**primeval waters, the waters of Noun**
	**nt**	n:t	**of**
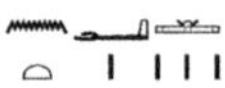	**nt-aw**	n:t-a:Z1-Y1:Z2	**custom, habit, routine**
	**nty**	n:t*y	**of**
	**ny**	n-i-i-A2	**'nyaah'** sound of crying baby
	**niwt**	O49:t*Z1	**city, town**
	**niwty**	O49:O49	**local, of the city**
	**niwtyw**	O49:t-tyw-A1:Z2	**townsmen**
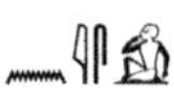	**nis**	n-i-s-A2	**to summon**
	**nar**	n:a-r-K1	**catfish**
	**nw**	n:U19-nw-w	**this, these**
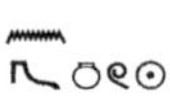	**nw**	n:U19-nw-Z7-N5	**time**
	**nw**	U19:t*Z1	**adze**

nw	n:U19-nw:Z7-V1-A24	**look after, see to**
nw	n:U19-nw-w-D54	**bring back**
nw	n:U19-nw-w-A17	**weak, limp**
nw	n:U19-nw-w-D54	**return**
nw	n:U19-nw-w-V1-A24	**collect, tend**
nwA	n-wA-A-D5	**look, see**
nwA	n:U19-nw-w-D5	**look, see**
nwy	n:U19-nw:Z7-i-i-n:n:n	**waters, water, flood**
nwyt	n:U19-nw-w-i-i-t:n:n:n	**wave**
nww	n:U19-nw-w-D4:Z2	**hunters**
nwH	n:U19-nw-H-V1	**rope, bind**
nwt	nw*t:N1-B1	**Nut (sky goddess)**
nwti	U19:nw*t-U19:U19	**the two adzes**
nwti	U20:nw*t-U20:U20	**the two adzes**
nwd	n:U19-nw-w-d:D54	**move crookedley, aslant**

nwdw: crookedness

nwd	n:U19-nw:d-W1	**ointment, perfume**
nk, ink	nw:k	**I, belongs to me**
nb	nb	**all, every, any, all kinds of**
nb	nb	**lord, master, possessor, owner, the lord**
nb	nb-A1	**lord, master, possessor, owner, the lord**
nb	nb:Z1	**lord, master, possessor, owner, the lord**

nbA n:b-bA-A-M3 **pole, var. nbi;**
nbiw: a linear measure longer than 1 cubit

nb-iwnt nb-iwn-n:t-O49 **Nebet-iunet** (woman's name)

nb-ir-xt nb-A41 **lord of action, lord of doing things**

nb-ir-xt nb-ir:x*t **lord of doing things**

nbyt n:b-i-i-t **the collar** S12

nbyt S13-i-i-t:O49 **Kom Ombo, town N. of Elephantine**

nb-tAwy nb-tA:tA **lord of the two lands**

nbw nbw:N33:Z2 **gold**

nbw nbw:N33*N33*N33 **gold**

nbwy G139-E147 **the Two Lords (Horus and Seth)**

nbw-kA-w-ra <-N5-nbw-kA*kA:kA-> **Nebw-ka-u-ra** (Amenotep II)

nbs n:b*s-M1 **Christ's thorn, Nebek tree**

nb-sny nb-z:n-i-i-A52 **Nebseny** (man's name)

nbt nb:t*Z1 **basket**

HAw-nbwt: HA-A-nb:t*Z1-A1*B1:Z2 **the Haw-Nebwet, probably the inhabitants of Greece; var:**

nbt nb:t **lady, possessor, owner**

nbt-Hwt nb:t-Hwt-t:O1-B1 **the goddess Nephtys**

nbty G16 **The Two Ladies**

tA-nbt-kpny: t-A-nb:t-kp:n:y-N25-B1 **Lady of Byblos**

nbt-nni-nsw nb:t-sw-t:n-A17-n:n:O49-B1 **Nebet-neni-nesw** (woman's name)

nbt S13-t:O49 **Ombos, near Tukh in U.E.**

nbdw-qdw n:b-d:w-D3:N33A-qd-d:nw-Y1v-T14-A1-Z3 **perverse of character, epithet given to foreign enemies**

npnpt n:p-n:p-t-S28 **hem** (of garment)

npri n:p:r-i-M33A **the corn-god Nepri**

nprt n:p-r:t-N23:Z1 **edge, brim** (of sheet of water)

nf n:f **that, those**

nf n:f-G37 **nonsense, wrong**

nfA n:f-A-N31 **that, those**

nfA n:f-A **that, those**

nfa n:f:a-D54 **remove, take away**

nfw P5-w-A24 **skipper**

nf-n n:f-n **those**

nfr nfr **zero**

nfr nfr-f:r **good, fine, fair, nice, kind, happy**

nfr nfr-f:r **not at all** (rare paticle):

nfrA nfr-f:r-A **not at all, not even**

nfryt nfr-f:r-i-i-t:V1*Z1 **tiller rope**

nfryt nfr-f:r-i-i-t **end**

nfrw nfr-w-G37:Z2 **shortage**

nfrw nfr-nfr-nfr-Z1:O1 **innermost rooms**

nfrt nfr-f:r:t **a good thing, good**

nfrty nfr-f:r-t:y-Y1:A1 **Neferty** (a man's name)

nft n:f:t-A24 **loose, slacken**

nftft n:f-t:f-t:D54 **to leap**

nA n:A-a **who? what?**

nm n:T34*m-D38 **who? what?**

nm n:T34*m-T34-Z1 **knife**

nmt n:T34*m-t-T29 **place of slaughter**

nmt T29-t:O1 **place of slaughter**

nma n-nm-m-a-A2 **to show partiality, to be partial, to be one sided**

nmi n:nm*m-i-O5:D54 **traverse**

Nmiw-Sa: Sand-farers, Beduins

nmi n:nm*m-i-O5-A2 **cry aloud**

nma n:nm*m-a-A2 **partially, show partiality**

nmH nm-n:m-H-A17-G37-A1 **poor man, orphan, waif**

nmH nm-n:m-H-A17-G37 **poor man, orphan, waif**

nms n:nm*m-s-S28 **Nemes, the royal headress**

nmst n:nm*m-s-t:W23 **jug (for water)**

nmty-nxt G7A:t*y-A24-A1 **Nemty-nakhet** (man's name)

nmi n:T34*m-i-D41:D54 **travel (by foot)**

nmi-Sa: sand travellors (Bedouins)

nmtt n:nm*m-t:t-D54:Z2 **steps, walk**

nmtt	D54-t:Z2	**steps, walk**
nmtt	D54-t:Z1	**steps, walk**
nmtt	D54*D54:D54	**steps, walk**
nn	D35:n	**not, without a..., not having a...**
nn-n	nn-n	**these, this, here**
nn	nn	**these, this**
Nini-nsw	sw-t:n-A17-n:n:O49-B1	**Heracleopolis Magna**

(City of the Royal Child). Capital during the 9th and 10th Dynasties. Capital of the 12th nome of Egypt, near modern day Beni Suef.

nni	nn-n:n-A7	**be tired, slothful**

nniw: wearyness

nnw	nw*nw*nw:N1	**primeval waters, the Nun**
nnm	n:n-nm-m-G37	**to err, go wrong, transgress**
nnSm	nn-N40-m-F51	**spleen**
nnSm	D35:n-N40-m-F51	**spleen**
nnk	n:n:k	**belongs to me, on my part**
nrw	n:r-w-G14-Z2:.	**fear, dread, awe**
nrAw	n:r-Aw-w-F27	**ibex**
nrt	n:r:t-G39	**vulture**
nrt	n:r-G14-t	**vulture**
nri	n:r-A24	**be in terror**
nrw	n:r-w-G14-A24-Z3	**terror**
nrw	n:r-w-H4:Z2	**terror**

nhy-n n:h-y:G37-N33:Z2-n **a little, some, a few**

nhw n:h-Z7-G37 **loss**

nhm n:h-m-A2 **to shout**

nhrn n:h-r:n:N25 **Naharin (Mitanni)**

(a country around the great bend of the river Euphrates)

nht n:h*t-M1 **sycamore**

nht n:h*t-O1 **shelter**

nhy n:h-y:G37-N33:Z2 **little, few**

nhw n:h-w-G37 **loss, need**

nhp n:h*p-N5 **rise early**

nhpw: early morning

nhm n:h-m-A2 **jubilate**

nhryn n:h-r:y-n:N25 **Nahrin, Mitanni, a kingdom East of the Euphrates river**

nhs n:h-s-U40-D5 **to wake up**

nH nH-Z1-G39 **guinea-fowl**

nH n:nH-H-A2 **prayer**

nHA n-H-HA-A-Aa2 **hard, rough, dangerous**

nHA n-HA-A-A24 **terrifying, terrible**

nHb nH-H-b-Z9 **yoke together, unite**

nHbt nH-H-b-t:F51 **neck**

nHbt nH-H-b-t:M10 **lotus bud**

nHp nH-H-p:O39 **potter's wheel**

nHm n:N41-m-A24 **to rescue, save, to take away, carry off, to take out, to withdraw**

nHm n:N41-m-a **to rescue, save**

nHmn n:N41-m-a:n **surely, indeed**

nHri n:Hr:r-i **Nehri** (a man's name)

nHH n-nH-H-H-N5 **forever, eternity**

nHsi nH-H-s-A1 **Nubian**

nHsy nH-H-s-y-A13 **Nubian**

nHsy T14-s-y **Nubian**

nHdt nH-H-d:t-F18 **tooth, molar**

nx n:x-D40 **defend, protect**

nxw: protector

nx n:x-A2 **pitiful**

nx.wy n:x-A2-w-y **how grevious!**

nxAw n:x-xA-A-Z7-K1 **pendant (shaped like a fish)**

nxb n:x-b-Z9 **open up (mine, fields)**

nxb n:x-b-Z9:N23 **newly opened up field**

nxbt n:x-b-t:Z9-Y1:Z2 **protocal, titulary**

nxb M22-b-nw:O49 **Nekheb, El-Kab, Eileithyias, a town in Upper Egypt**

nxHbt M22-b-nw:t-G15 **Nekhebet, the vulture goddess**

nxn O47:O49 **Nekhen, Kom el-Ahmar, Hieraconpolis, a town in Upper Egypt**

r-nxn: r:O48*O49 **mouth of Nekhen**

minw-nxn: A47-O48:O49 **herdsman (ruler) of Nekhen**

nxn n:x:n-A17 **be young, child**

nxnw, nxnt: childhood

nxxw n:x*x-w-S45 **flagellum**

nxxw S45-Z1 **flagellum**

nxt n:xt:x*t-D40 **strong, mighty, victorious, stiff**

nxt A24 **strong, mighty, victorious, stiff, victory**

nxt n:xt-x:t-A24 **victory, be strong, mighty, victorious**

nxtw: victory, hostages, strongholds

nxt n:xt:x*t-A24-A1 **champion**

nxt-Hr n:xt:x*t-A24-Hr-Z1 **violent, violent man**

nxtw n:xt:x*t **strength, force, power, victory**

nXnm n-W9-W9 **ritual oil, jug for ritual oil**

ns ns:F51*Z1 **tongue**

nswt n:ns-z:Z7-t-Q7-Z3 **(tongue of) flame**

imy-r F20 **overseer**

nsw-mnTw mn:n-T-w-n:ns-sw-w-A1 **Nisu-Montu** (name)

nsw, nswt sw-t:n **king**

nsyt sw-i-t-i **kingship**

nswyt sw-i-i-t:Y1 **kingship**

nswt biti sw:t-bit:t **King of Upper and Lower Egypt**

	**nsb**	n:ns-b	**lick**
	**nsr**	n:ns-s-r-Q7	**to burn, blaze**
nsrt: flame			
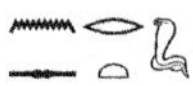	**nsrt**	n:z-r:t-I12	**the uraeus goddess**
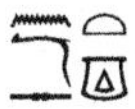	**nst**	n:ns:z-t:W11	**seat (of office)**
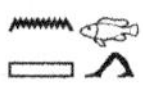	**nS**	n:S-K5:D54	**supplant, drive away, replace**
	**nSmt**	n:S-m-t:P1	**sacred bark of Osiris at Abydos**
	**nSmt**	n:S-m-t:K6	**fish scale**
	**nSmt**	K6	**fish scale**
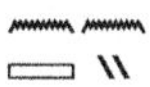	**nSny**	n:S-n:y	**storm**
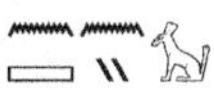	**nSny**	n:S-n:y-E20	**storm, tempest, rage**
	**nSp**	n:S-p-D19-A2	**breathe**
	**nqwt**	n:q-w-t-N33:Z2	**notched sycamore figs**
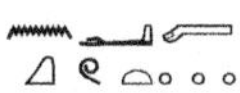	**nqawt**	n:q-a:Z7*t-D51:N33A	**notched sycamore figs**
	**nqm**	n:q-m-C6	**pain, sorrow**
	**nqdd**	n-qd-d:d-D5	**sleep**
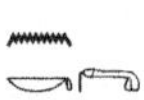	**nk**	n:k-D53	**copulate**
	**nkA**	n:k-A-A2	**reflect**
	**ngAw**	n:g-A-w-E1	**steer**
	**ngw**	n:g*Z7-E1	**long-horned bull, ox**
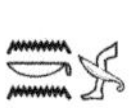	**nkn**	n:k:n-D57	**harm, punishment, damage**
	**nkt**	n:k-t:Z9	**a little, a trifle**

	**ng**	n:g-E1	**a species of bull**
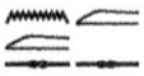	**ngsgs**	n:gs:z-gs:z	**overflow**
	**nt**	n:t-R24v-B1	**Neith, the goddess of Sais**
	**nt**	n:t-S3	**the red crown of Lower Egypt**
	**nt**	n:t-S4	**the red crown of Lower Egypt**
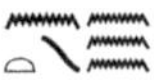	**nt**	n:t*Z5-N35A	**water**
	**nt-a**	n:t-a:Z1-Y1:Z2	**custom, observances, practice**
	**nty**	n:t*y	**that, which, who**
	**ntyw**	n:t-G4-Z2:.	**those who are/were**
	**ntyw**	n:t-G4	**those who are/were**
	**ntyw**	n:t-G4-A1:Z2	**those who are/were**
	**ntyw-im**	n:t-G4-Z2:.-i-m	**those who are there**

(the dead, in the world of the afterlife)

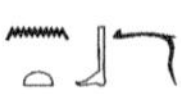	**ntb**	n:t-b-F20	**be parched**
	**nt-pw**	n:t-p:Z7	**it is the fact that**
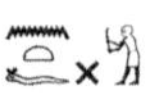	**ntf**	n:t:f-Z9-A24	**loose, slacken**
	**ntf**	n:t:f	**belongs to im**
	**ntf, nty.f**	n:t:f	**which he...**
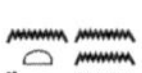	**ntf**	n:t:f-N35A	**irrigate, water**
	**ntf**	n:t:f-Z9-A24	**loose, slacken**
	ntt	n:t*t	**that, which, that which, who, that which exists, that which is, she who is**

m-a-ntt: 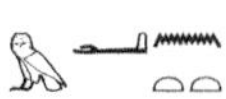 m-a:.-n:t*t **seeing that**

r-ntt: r-n:t*t **to the effect that**

Hr-ntt: Hr:Z1-n:t*t **because, on account of the fact that, to the effect that**

Dr-ntt: Dr:r-n:t*t **because, since**

ntf	n:t:f	**he, belong to him**
ntry	nTr-t:r:y-Y1v	**be divine**
nts	n:t-s	**she, belongs to her**
ntsnw	n:t-s-n:Z2	**they, belongs to them**
ntS	n:t:S-n:n:n	**to sprinkle**
ntk	n:t:k	**you, belongs to you** (masc.)
ntk, nty.k	n:t:k	**which you...**
ntt	n:t*t	**that**
ntt	n:t*t	**you (fem.)**
ntT	n:t:T	**you, belongs to you** (fem.)
ntTnw	n:t-T:n:Z2	**you, belongs to you** (plur.)
nTr	nTr-Z1	**god**

Hm-nTr: nTr-Hm **god's servant, priest**

nTrt	nTr-r:t-I12	**goddess**
ndb	n:d-b-D51:D40	**cover, overlay**
ndbwt	n:d-b-w-t:N23-Z3	**area, extent**
nD	Aa27	**save, protect**
nD	Aa27-nw-A2	**to ask, enquire, seek advice**
nD	nD-nw:a	**grind, miller**

nD	nD-nw:D40	**save**
nD	nD-nw-S28	**thread**
nDA	n-DA-A-F10	**be parched, stifled**
nDyt	n:D-i-i-t-G37:Z2	**baseness, bad character**
nDb, ndb	n:D-b-A2	**to sip**
ndbyt	n:d-b-i-i-t-S28	**reefs (of a sail)**
nD-xrt	nD-nw-A2-x:r*t-Y1:Z2	**to greet, Greetings!**
nDm	M29	**sweet** (of flavour, odour)
nDm	n:D-nDm-m-Y1:.	**sweet** (of flavour, odour)
nDm	M29-M1	**species of tree**
nDnD	nD-nw-nD-nw-A2	**converse, take counsel**
nDri	n:Dr:r-A24	**seize, catch hold of, hold firm**
nDrt	n:Dr:r-t-A24	**captivity, imprisonment**
nDHt	n:D-H-t:F18	**tusk**
nDHyt	n:D-H-i-i-t-F18:Z2	**tusk, teeth**
nDs	n:D-s-G37	**small, little, dim**
nDs	G37	**be small, poor, feeble**
nDs	n:D-s-G37-A1	**poor man, commoner**
nDsw	n:D-s-w-G37-A1:Z2	**poverty, low status**
nDt	n:D-t*Z1-A1:Z2	**subjects, serfs**
nDt	n:D:t*Z1	**subjects, serfs**
nDty	nD-nw*t:y:D40	**protector, savior**

r

	r	r	phonetic sound **r**
	r	r	**to, towards, concerning, regarding, with relation to, at, from, into, more than, against, so that, until,**
	r	r:Z1	**mouth, statement, words, opening, entrance**
	r	r:Z1-G39	**a species of goose**
st-r		st-t:O1-r:Z1	**occasion for speech, autority**
r-Aw		r:Z1-Aw-w-N25	**Turah, white limetson quarries**
tp-r		tp:Z1-r:Z1	**utterance**
	r-Aw	r:Z1-wA-A-t:N31	**path, place of passage**
	r.i	r:A1	**to I, to me**
	r-a	r:a*Z1	**place, state**
	ra	r:a-N5	**sun, day**
	ra	r:a-A40	**Ra** (the sun god)
	ra-nb	N5:nb	**every day**
	ra-Axty	G9-N27:N27:.:.	**Ra-Harakty**
	r-awi	r:a-w-Y1	**activity**
	r-awy	r:Z1-a:a	**hands, activity of hands**
	ra-wsr	N5-wsr-s-r:D40-A1	**Ra-weser** (man's name)
	r-a-xt	r:a*Z1-xt:t*Z1	**war, combat**
	rwt	r:w-t:N1	**gateway, outside**

rwty: double doors

r-wAt r:Z1-wA-A-t:N31 **path, opening of the path**

rwyt rw:r-i-i-t:O1 **gateway, place of judgement**

rwyt U13-i-i-t:O1 **gateway, place of judgement**

r-pw r:Z1-p-w **or, either**

r-pr r:Z1-pr:Z1 **temple, house of utterance**

r-pr r:pr:Z1 **temple, house of utterance**

r-pDt r:Z1-pD:t*Z1-T14-A1:Z2 **foreign bowmen**

rwi r-w-i-D54 **to depart, get away, to leave, to go away, to escape, to drive out, eliminate**

rwi r:w-i-D54-A33 **wander**

rwt r:E23-w-t:O1 **gate**

rwty r-w-t*y:N1 **outside**

rwd r:w-d:O40 **stairway**

rwD T12 **cord**

rwd r-w-d:T12 **bow string**

rwd r-w-d:T12-Y1v **hard, vigorous, flourishing**

rwd, rwD T12-A24 **firm**

rwdt r-w-d:t-T12-O39 **hard stone, sandstone**

rwD T12:Y1 **firm**

rwD r:d-T12-M32-Y1v **firm**

rwD r-wD-D-T12 **to be strong, firm, to flourish, prosper, to succeed**

rwD	T12-w-D40	**control, administer, controller, executor**
rpa	r:p:a	**hereditary nobleman, prince**
rpatt, rt-pat, irt-pat	r:p-a:t*t	**princess**
rpyt	r:p-i-i-t-A53	**statue (of female)**
rf	r:f	**then, now**
rm	r-m-K5	**fish**
rmy	r-m-ir	**to cry, weep, weeper**
rmy	D9	**to cry, weep, weeper**
rmyt	r-m-i-i-t:D9	**tears, weeping**
rmw	r-m-Z7-K1:Z2	**fish**
rmn	r-mn:n-D41	**arm, shoulder, side**
rmn	r:mn-n:D41	**carry on shoulder**
rmn	D41	**measure of area, 1/2 aroura**
rmnn	r:mn-n:n-N25	**Lebanon**
rmn-n-iH	r-mn:n-D41:F51-n-E1	**side of beef**
rmT	r:T-A1	**people, person**
rmTt	r:T:t-A1*B1:Z2	**people**
rn	r:n	**name**
rn	r:n-A2	**name**
rn	r:n	**young (of cattle, antilopes etc.)**
rnn	r:n:n-A2	**praise, belaud**

rnnwt: jubilation

rnn	r:n:n-B6	**nurse, rear**
rnnwtt	r:n:n-w-t:t-I12	**Ernutet, the cobra goddess of the harvest**
rnpi	r:n:p-i-M7	**young, vigorous**
rnpt	rnp-t:Z1	**year**
rnpw	r:n:p-Z7-M6-A17	**young**
rnpwt	M7-M39:Z2	**vegetables and fruit**
rnpy	r:n:p-i-i-M4	**young, youthful**
rnsy	r:n-s-y-A1	**Rensy** (man's name)
rri	r:r-i-E12	**pig**

rrt: sow

rhn	r:h:n-D41	**to rely on, to trust in, to lean on**
rhni	r:h:n-D41:D40	**rest, rely, depend**
rhni	r:h:n-D56	**rest, rely, depend**
rhdt	r:r-d:t*W22	**jar, cauldron**
rHw	r-H-w-A1:Z2	**men, fellows**
rx	r:x-Y1	**to learn, find out, to know**
rx	r:x:Y1-A1	**learned man, scholar**
rx-nsw	sw-t:n-r:x:Y1	**king's acquaintance, lit. known of the king**
r-xt	r:Z1-X:t*Z1	**stomach, belly, mouth of the belly**
rxwt	G24:t-A1*B1:Z2	**subjects**
rxyt	r:x-i-i-t-G23-A1*B1:Z2	**people, common folk**

Transliteration	Code	Meaning
rxyt	r:x-i-i-t-A1*B1:Z2	**subjects**
rxs	r:x-s-T30:D40	**butcher, slaughter**
rxt	r:x:t-Y1:Z2	**knowledge, account, enumeration**
rxt	r:x*t-Y1v	**amount, number**
rxty	G50-t:y-A1	**fuller, washerwoman**
rs	r:z-T13-D4	**be wakeful**
rs	T13-D4	**be wakeful**
rsy	M24-N23	**southern**
rs-tp	rs-D5:D1*Z1	**vigilant**

rswt: dream; s-rs: awaken

Transliteration	Code	Meaning
rswt	r-s-w-t-U40-D4	**dream**
rssy	r-s-s-y:N31	**quite, entirely, at all**
rst	rs-t-A13	**foreign hordes**
r-sTAw	r:Z1-V3:N25	**necropolis under god Sokar of Memphis**
rS	r:S-D19-A2	**joyful, happy**
rSwt	r:S-w-t-D19-Y1v	**joy, a state of joy**
rq	r:q-D41	**oppose, revolt**
rqy	r:q-i-i-D41:D54-A14	**opponent**
rk	r:k-N5	**time, era, age**
rk	r:k	**then, now**
rkH	r:k-Q7	**burning, heat**
rkty	U31:t*y-A24	**baker**

rtH r:t-H-U31 **restrain**

rTnw r:T-n:nw*Z7-T14-G41-N25 **Retjenu (Lebanon)**

tnw, rtnw t:n-nw:Z7-T14-G41-N25 **Retjenu (Lebanon)**

rtH r:t-H-U31:D40 **restrain**

rtHty r:t-H-t:y-U31-A1 **baker**

rT r:T **but, now**

rTn r-T:n **but, now**

rTnw r:T-n:nw*w-N25 **Retjenu, Palestine and Syria**

rd r:d-D56 **foot**

rdwy D56-D56 **two feet**

tp-rd: tp:Z1-D56 **rules, order, principles**

rd r:d-O40 **stairway**

rd r:d-M32 **to grow, to flourish, to prosper**

rd M32-Y1v **to grow, to flourish, to prosper**

rd r:d-M32-Y1v **to grow, to flourish, to prosper**

rd r:d-T12 **to grow, to flourish, to prosper**

rdi r:X8 **to give, place, cause**

rdi r:D37 **to give, to put, to place, to appoint, to cause that someone (do something)**

rdi r:D41 **to give, place, cause**

rdy, dy di-Z1-i-i-Y1:Z2 **gift, gratuity**

rdiw, diw di-Z1-U9:Z2 **provisions, rations**

	**rd**	r:d-D56	**foot**
	**rdmt**	r:d-m-t:M2-Z3	**rushes**
	**r-DAyw**	r:Z1-DA-i-i-w-D40:Z2	**melee, time of battle**
	**rdi**	r:a	**to give, put, place, allow**
	**rDw**	r:N26-w-Aa2	**fluid**
	**rdDdt**	r:d-T12-Y1-Dd-d:t*B1	**Redjedet** (a woman's name)

h

h

h h phonetic sound **h**

h h*Z1:O1 **courtyard**

hA h-A **oh! ha!**

hAi h-A-D54 **to go down, descend, fall, attack**

hAw h-A-w-Y1:Z2 **vicinity, neighbourhood, time, reign, affairs, belongings**

hAw h-A-w-A1*B1:Z2 **neighbours, kindred**

hAb h-A-b-D54 **to send, send word**

hAk h-A-k:W3 **name of feast**

hAt h-A-t:N1 **ceiling, roof**

ht, hAyt h*t:N1 **portal**

hAyt h:Z1-A-i-i-t-O1:Z1 **portal**

hyt h-i-i-t:N1 **portal**

smsw-hyt: elder of the portal, usher in the palace

hi h-i-D53-A1 **husband**

hy h-i-i-D53:A1 **husband**

hAy h-A-i-i-D53:A1 **husband**

hi-ms h-i-ms-s-D54 **approaching in humble attitude**

hy h-i-i-A2 **hail**

hy-nw h-i-i-h:n-nw-w-A32 **jubilation, jubilate**

	**hb**	h-b-D54	**enter, penetrate into**
hbhb: explore, traverse			
	**hb**	h-b-G26	**ibis**
	**hb**	h-b-U13	**a plough**
	**hbi**	h-b-U13:D54	**to plough**
	**hbnt**	U13-n:t-W22	**a liquid measure**
	**hbnt**	h-b-n:t*W22	**a liquid measure**
	**hbny**	U13:n-y:M3	**ebony**
	**hp**	h*p:Y1	**law, custom**
	**hmt**	h-m-t:N18	**fare, payment to ferryman**
	**hmhmt**	h-m-h-m-t-A2	**roaring, war-cry**
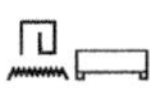	**hn**	h:n-Q5	**box, chest**
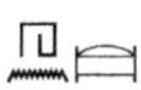	**hn**	h:n-Q6	**box, chest**
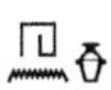	**hn**	h:n-W23	**jar, hin (measure)**
	**hnw, hin**	h:n-nw-w-W23	**liquid measure 0.5 litres**
	**hnw**	h:n-nw-w-A8	**jubilation**
	**hnw**	h:n-nw-w-A1*B1:Z2	**neighbours, associates**
	**hnn**	h:n:n-D1	**nod, bow, attend to, rely**
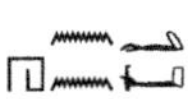	**hnn**	h-n:n-D41:D40	**nod, bow, attend to, rely**
	**hri, hr**	h:r-Y1v	**be content, pleased, quiet**
hrt: contentment, quiet			
	**hrw**	h:r-w-N5	**day, daytime**

	**hrw**	N5:Z1	**day, daytime**
	**hrw**	h-r-Z7-Y1	**pleasing, to be pleased, satisfied**
	**hrp**	h:r-p-N35A	**sink, be subverged**
hrp-ib: suppress thoughts			
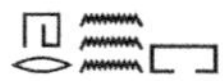	**hrmw**	h:r-N35A-O1	**enclosure for poultry, pen**
	**hh**	h:h-Q7	**blast (of fire), hot breath**
	**hq**	h:q-Z5	**to break out?**
	**hqs**	h:q-s-G37	**be deficient, stint**
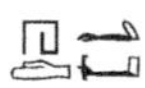	**hd**	h:d-D41:D40	**punish, defeat, (victorious) attack**
	**hdmw**	h:d-N35A-M3	**footstool**

H

H

H	H	phonetic sound **H**, aspirated h
HA	N25:R12-A40	**the desert-god Ha**
HA	H-A-A2	**would (you) please... would that! wish**
HA	H-A	**would (you) please... would that! wish**
HA	HA-A-D1	**behind, around, back of head**
HA	HA-A-O1	**behind, around**
HA	HA-A	**one who is behind, around**
HAt	H-A-t:O1	**tomb**
HAt-ib	HA-A-t-Aa2:Z2-F34:Z1	**grief, sadness**
HAw	H-A-w-Y1:Z2	**wealth, excess, exageration**
HAt (see AHt)	H-A-t:N23	**field**
HAt-sp	M4-t:O50	**regnal year**
HAt	HAt:t*Z1	**front, forepart, forehead, vanguard of army, beginning, foremost, the best of**
HAt-a	HAt:a	**beginning**
HAti-a	HAt:a-A1	**high official, 'one with hand in front'**
HAi	H-HA-A-S28	**naked, undressed, make naked, reveal**
HAi	HA-A-G37	**naked, undressed, make naked, reveal**
HAayt	HA-A-a-i-i-t-A24	**strife, civil war**
HAy	HA-A-i-i-S28	**naked**

HAwt: nakedness

HAb	W4-N5	**festival**
HAp	HA-A-p:V6-A24	**concealed**

HApw-xt: discreet

HAp	HA-A-p-S28-A24	**conceal, hide**
HAm	HA-A-m-G51-A24	**catch fish, fowl etc.**
HAqt	HA-A-q:t-D40:Z2	**plunder**
HAq	HA-A-q-A24	**to plunder, plunder**
HAty	HAt:t*y-F34	**heart, thought, breast**
HAtyw	HAt:t*Z1-F34:Z2	**hearts, thoughts**
HAtyw	HA-A-w-S28	**linen**
HAty-a	HAt:a	**count, regional governor, mayor**
HAtt	HAt:t*t-V1	**bow warp of ship**
HiHi, HHy	H-H-y:D54	**to seek**
Hii	H-A24	**strike, beat, drive in (mooring post), tread (a road)**
Hii	H-A25-A24	**strike, beat, drive in (mooring post), tread (a road)**
Hyt	H-A19-i-i-t:N35A	**rain**
Haq	HA-q:D40	**to plunder, plunder, booty**
Ha	H-a:F51	**flesh, body**
HaA	H-aAv-A-G37	**child, lad**
Hai	H-a-A28-Y1	**to be joyous, rejoice**
Hai	H-a-A28	**become aroused, excited**

Transliteration	Codes	Meaning
Ha	H-a:P1	**ship**
Haw	H-a-w-P1:Z2	**ships, fleet**
Hapy	H-a:p-y:N36-N35A	**inundation (of Nile)**
Hapy	H-a:p-n:n:n	**Nile, Hapy (the Nile god)**
Hap-aA	H-a:p-n:n:n-aA:a-A-Y1	**high Nile**
Hat	H-a:D133*t	**wick (D133)**
HaDA	H-a-DA-A-A24	**pillage, plunder**
Hp-Df	H-p:N36-D:f	**Hep-Djefa** (man's name)
Hw	H-w-F18-G7	**Hu, deity personifying Auhtoritative Utterance**
HwA	H-wA-A-Aa2	**rot, decay**
Hwa	H-w-a:G37	**be short**
Hwt	Hwt-t:O1	**estate, large building, tomb**
Hwt-aAt	O8-t:O1	**castle**
Hwt-wart	Hwt-t:O1-D56-t:O49	**Avaris (Hyksos capital)**
Hwt-nbw	**Enclosure of Gold**	
Hwt-nTr	nTr-Hwt-t:O1	**temple**
Hwt-nTr	nTr-Hwt	**temple**
Hwt-Hr	Hwt-Hr:r-C9	**Hathor (goddess)**
Ht-Hr	O10	**Hat-hor (goddess)**
Hwt-kA	Hwt-t:kA-O1	**soul-house**
Hwi	H-A25-A24	**to beat, strike, tread, drive in (stake)**
Hwy	H-A25-i-i-n:n:n	**well-trodden, beaten (path)**

Hwyt	H-A25-i-i-t:n:n:n	**rain**
Hwy	H-w-y	**please! would that!**
Hwy-a	H-w-y-A2-A	**would that!**
Hwn	H-wn:n-A18	**youthful vigour, refreshed**
Hwrw	H-wr:r-w-G37-A1	**poor man, humble man**
Hwtf	H-w-t:f:D40	**to plunder, rob**
Hb	W4	**festival**
Hb	H-b-W3	**feast, festival**
Hb	H-W3-b	**to triumph**
Hb	H-W3-b-A24	**mourn**
HbAbA	H-b-bA-A-b-bA-A-D54	**to waddle**
Hbs	H-b-s-S28	**to clothe, be clothed, put on garment, cover**
Hbs-Hr	H-b-s-S28-Hr	**to be indifferent, infifference, literally: cover the face ie look the other way**
Hbs	H-b-s-S28	**garment, clothing, clothes**
Hbs	S28:Z2	**garment, clothing, clothes**
Hbsw	H-b-s-w-S28-Z3	**clothhing, clothes**
Hb-sd	W4-s-d:N20-O23	**jubilee, Sed-festival**
Hbt	H-b-t:W3-V12	**ritual book**
Hp	H-p:Aa5-E1	**Apis bull**
Hpt	Aa5:t-P8	**oar**
Hpt	Aa5:t*Z1	**oar**

Hpt H-p:t-D32:a **to embrace**

Hpt H-p:t-D32 **to embrace, embrace**

Hp-wy S36-p-S36 **Hepuy, a deity personifying te king's two sunnshades**

Hp-Df H-p:N36-D:f **Hep-djefa** (man's name)

HfAw H-f-A-w-I14 **snake, serpent**

HfAw H-f:Aw-w-I14 **snake**

HfAt H-f-A-t:I14 **female serpent**

HfAt H-f-A-t-A16 **crawling**

Hfn I8 **100,000**

Hm Hm-Z1-G7 **incarnation**

Hm N41-m **assuredly, indeed**

Hm N42-m-a **and, also (particle)**

Hm N42-m-A24 **and, also (particle)**

Hm U36-Z1-A1 **male slave, servant**

Hm Hm-Z1-A42 **Majesty**

Hm N41-m-D52 **a poltroon (an ignoble or total coward, a dastard, a mean-spirited wretch)**

Hmi N41-m-D55 **flee, retire**

Hma N41-m:a **to be sure, surely, indeed**

Hmw Hm-Z7-A1 **servant**

Hmw N42-m-Z7-P10 **rudder**

Hmw U26-w-A1 **craftsman**

Transliteration	Code	Meaning
Hmww	Hm-w-w	**washerman, fuller**
Hmwti	U25-w-t-A1	**craftsman**
Hm-nTr	nTr-Hm	**priest, 'god's servant'**
Hm-xt	N41-m-xt:x*t-D55	**to retreat**
Hmsi	N42:z-A1	**to sit down, reside**
Hms	N42:z-A1	**seat**
Hm-kA	D31	**soul-priest, ka-priest**
Hmt	Hm-t-B1	**servant**
Hmt	N41:t-B1	**wife, woman**
Hmt	N34:Z1-N33:Z2	**bronze, copper**
Hmt-nsw	sw-N41:t	**Wife of the King**
Hmt-nsw-wrt	sw-N41:t-wr:t	**Great Wife of the King**
Hmw	N41-m-Z7-P10	**steering oar**
Hmw-ib	U24-w-A24-F34:Z1	**clever, skilful**
Hmww	U24-w-w	**craftsman**
Hm	Hm-A1	**servant, slave**
Hmt	Hm-t-B1	**female servant, slave**
Hm-kA	D31-A1	**soul priest, *ka* priest**

Order of priests who supervised the funerary cult of the deceased and supplied offerrings to the deceased person's *ka* (soul).

Transliteration	Code	Meaning
Hm	U36-Z1	**Majesty**
Hmt	U25-t:Z1-Y1	**skill, craft, art**
Hmt	U24-t:Y1	**skill, craft, art**

Hmwt U24-w:t-A1:Z2 **body of craftsmen**

Hmt U24-t:Z1-N33:Z2 **glass flux**

An ingredient used in glass making.

Hmww U25-w-w-A1 **artist, artisan, craftsman**

HmAt H-mA-A-t-U32-N33:Z2 **salt**

HmAgt H-mA-A-g:t-N33:Z2 **a red stone from Nubia, almost certainly garnet**

Hmsi N41:z-A7 **to sit, to live,** *Hmsi m* (to live, to dwell in a place)

Hmsi N41:z-A1 **sit down, sit, dwell, besiege**

Hn H-Hn:n-V36-D54 **to hurry, rush** (to a place)

Hn H-Hn:n-D54 **rush, hurry, attack**

Hn H-U8:n-V36 **a receptacle given to a temple**

Hn H-Hn:n-V36-Y1v **commend, command, take care of**

Hni H-Hn:n-i-M2 **rush plant**

Hna H-n:a **with, together with, and**

Hn H-n **with, together with, and**

Hnaw H-n:a:Z2 **therewith, together with them**

Hnw M2:n-nw*Z7:Y1-Z2 **vessels, property, goods**

Hnw H-Hn:n-nw-w-W22:Z1 **vessels, property, goods**

Hnw H-U8:n-nw-w-G10 **sacred bark of the god Sokar**

Hnwt H-nw:t-B1 **mistress**

Hnmmt	N8-G18-t-A1*B1:Z2	**humanity, the sun-folk of Heliopolis**
Hnmnm	H:n-nm-m-nm-m-D54	**to creep**
Hnn	H-Hn:n-n:D53	**phallus**
Hnn	H-n:n-U8-Z1	a **hoe**
Hnn	H-Hn:n:n-D53	**phallus**
Hnnw	H-mr-n:n:D53-w	**phallus**
Hnqt	H-q:t-W23	**beer**
Hnqyt	H-Hn:n-k:i*i-t:D41-S28-Z1	**bed**
HnHn	H-Hn:n-H-Hn:n-D55	**hinder, be detained**
Hns	H-Hn:n-s-G37	**narrow**
Hnskt	H-Hn-s-k:t-D3	**lock of hair**
Hnqt	H-q:t-W23	**beer**
Hnqt	W23	**beer**
Hnnkyt	H-Hn-n:k-i-i-t:D41-S28-Z1	**bed, couch**
Hnk	H-Hn:n-k:D38	**present, offer**
Hnkt	D38:t:W24*W24*W24	**offerings (of meat and drink)**
Hnt	H-M2:n-t:Y1	**occupation**
Hnt	V36-t	**occupation**
Hnt	H-n:t-W10	**cup**
Hnt	H-Hn:n-t:N36	**swampy lake**
Hnt	H-Hn:n-t-F16	**horn**

Hnt H-Hn:n-t:I3 **be greedy, covetous**

Hnty H-M2:n-t:Z4A-V36-N31:N31 **period, end**

Hnty V36-V36 **period, end**

Hr Hr:Z1 **face**

Hr Hr:r-N31 **be far**

Hr Hr:r-Aa19:N31 **be far**

Hrw-r N31-r **apart from, besides**

Hr G5-A40 **Horus** (the falcon god)

Hr G5 **Horus** (the falcon god)

Hr H-Hr:r-Aa19-A24 **prepare**

Hr-Axty G5-N18:N18:.:. **Harakhety, Horus of the Horizon**

Hr-nxny G13-O47:O49 **Horus of Nekhen**

Hrrt Hr:r-r:t-M2 **flower**

Hr-dd.f G5-D37:D37-f-A50 **Har-dedef** (a prince)

Prince Hardedef

Prince Hardedef, son of Khufu who built the Great Pyramid at Giza, was revered by later generations as a sage. The Instruction in Wisdom is accredited to him.

Hr Hr:Z1 **face, surface**

Hr Hr:Z1 **on, upon, on account of, because, concerning, about, and, in addition to**

Hr-ib Hr:Z1-F34:Z1 **in the middle of**

Hry-ib Hr:r-y:F34 **middle**

Hry-ib Hr*ib:r **who is at (a town)**

Hryt Hr:r-i-i-t:Aa19-D40:Z2 **dread**

Hr-awy Hr:Z1-a:Z1-w-y **immediately**

Hrw Hr:r-w-N1 **upper part**

Hr-m Hr:Z1-m:a **Why? on account of what?**

Hr-ntt Hr:Z1-n:t*t **because, on account of the fact that**

Hr-xw Hr:Z1-x*x:x **except, apart from**

Hr-nb Hr*Z1:nb-A1*B1:Z2 **everyone**

Hrst Hr:r-s-t-N33:Z2 **carnelian**

Hr-sy-iSst Hr-Z1-O35-i-V6:z-t-A2 **why?**

Hr-tp Hr:Z1-tp:Z1 **on top of**

Hry H-Hr:r-N31 **go far away**

Hry Hr:r-N1 **upper, who/which is above/over**

Hry Hr:r-y:N1 **who/which is over, upper, chief**

Hry N1 **who/which is over, upper, chief**

Hry Hr:r-y:N1-A24 **who/which is over, upper, chief**

Hry-ib Hr:r-F34:Z1 **middle**

Hry-a Hr:r-a:G37-Z3 **arrears**

Hry-pr N1-O1:Z1-A1 **chief of the household staff**

Hry-pr Hr:r-y:O1-Z1-A1 **chief of the household staff**

Hry-S.f Hr:r-N1-S:N23-f-G7 **He-who-is-upon-his-lake, Arsaphes, the ram-god of Heracleopolis**

Hry-Sa: Beduins, lit. those-upon-the-sand

Hry-tA Hr:r-N1-tA:N23*Z1-A1 **survivor** (of a deceased person)

Hry-tp Hr:r-tp:Z1 **who/which is upon, chief**

Hry-tp Hr:tp-A1 **chief, nomarch**

Hry-tp Hr:r:N1-tp-Z1 **headman, master**

Hrw G5 **Horus**

Hrw Hr:r-Aa19-A24-Z3A **plot, plotting**

Hrty Hr:r-t:y-D54 **to travel overland**

HH C11 **Heh, one of te eight Heh gods who hold the sky aloft**

HH C11 **million** (cardinal number), **a great number**

HHy H-H-y:D54 **to search (for), seek out**

Xry-Hbt H-Xr:r-b-W3-A1 **lector priest**

Hry-Dba Hr:r-D50-E1 **hornless cattle,**

'One upon the finger'

Hrt Hr:r-t:N1 **heaven, sky, upland**

Hrt Hr:r-t:N31 **road**

Hrt Hr:r-t:N25 **upland tomb**

Hryw M4-t:Z4B-Z3A-Hr-w **the five epagomenal days**

Hry-pr Hr:r-y:O1 **menial**

Hs H-s-Aa2:Z2 **excrement**

Hs H-W14-s-P5 **freeze**

Hs H-W14-s-D54 **turn back, turn in homeward direction**

HsA H-z:G39 **wild**

 **Hsi** H-W14-z-A2 **bless, to praise, honour, favour**

 **Hsi** H-W14-s-A2 **sing**

Hsw: singer (masc.)

Hsyt: singer (fem.)

 **Hsi-ti** H-W14:z-A2-ti-i **may it please you**

 **Hswt** Hz-w-t:Z2 **blessing**

 **Hst** H-W14-z:t-A2 **favour, praise**

 **Hst** W14-t:Z1 **water pot**

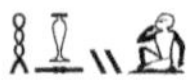 **Hsy** H-W14:z-y-A2 **to sing**

 **Hsy** H-W14-A2 **to sing**

 **Hsyw** H-W14-s-i-i-Z7-A2-A1 **singer**

 **Hsb** H-s-b-Aa2:Y1 **to calculate, reckon, count**

 **Hsb** Z9-b **to calculate, reckon**

 **Hsb** Aa2:Z1 **fracture** (in bone)

 **Hsbt** H-s-b-t-I15 **worm**

 **Hsbt** M4-t:O50 **regnal year**

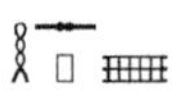 **Hsp** H-z:p-N24 **garden**

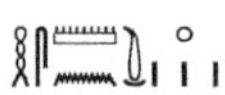 **Hsmn** H-s-mn:n-U32-N33:Z2 **natron,** also **bronze, amethyst**

 **Hsmn** U32-N34:N33A **bronze**

 **Hsmn** U32-n:N33:Z2 **natron,** also **bronze, amethyst**

Natron is a naturally occuring salt deposit used as an embalminng and cleaning agent.

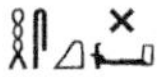	**Hsq**	H-s-q-Z9:D40	**to sever, cut off**
	**Hsq**	H-s-q:T30	**to sever, cut off**
	**Hnqt**	H-q:t-W22	**beer**
	**HqA**	HqA-q-A-A1	**ruler**
	**HqA**	HqA-A1	**ruler**
	**HqA**	HqA-Z1	**ruler**
	**HqA-Hwt**	HqA-O6-t:O49-A1	**local ruler, mayor, district governor**
	**HqAt**	HqA-q:t-U9	**heqat,** a dry measure of 4.54 litres.
	**HqAt**	U11	**heqat,** a dry measure of 4.54 litres
	**HqAt**	T14-U9	**heqat,** a dry measure of 4.54 litres
	**HqAt**	U12	**heqat,** a dry measure of 4.54 litres
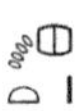	**HqAt**	U9:t*Z1	**heqat,** a dry measure of 4.54 litres
	**HqAt**	U9	**heqat,** a dry measure of 4.54 litres
	**Hqr**	H-q:r-G37-A2	**to be hungry, to fast**
	**Hqrw**	H-q:r-A2-A1	**hungry man**
	**Hqr**	H-q:r-G37-A2	**hunger**
	**Hqn**	H-k:n:Y1	**(he who is) praised**
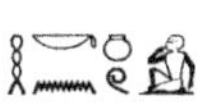	**Hqnw**	H-k:n-nw:Z7-A2	**praise**
	**Hqnw**	H-k:n-nw:Z7-N33:Z2	**Hknw-oil** (a sacred oil)

Hekenw was sweet scented oil produced for 'anointing the divine limbs' and took a total of 365 days to prepare.

Hqt H-q:t-I7 **Heqet, the frog goddess**

Hqt S38-t:Z1 **HqAt sceptre**

Hqt H-q:t-S38 **HqAt sceptre**

HqA S38-q-A-Y1v **to rule**

HqA S38-q-A1 **chieftain**

HqA S38-q-A42 **ruler, the king**

HqA-Hwt S38-O6 **village headman**

HqAt S38-q:t-U9 **Heqat measure, a gallon**

Hqr H-q:r-A2 **be hungry**

Hqrw: hunger

HkA H-kA-A-A2 **magic**

HkAy: magician

HkAw H-kA-A-A2-Y1:Z2 **magic**

HkAw H-kA-A-A2-Y1:Z2 **magic**

Hkn H-k:n **exult**

Hkn H-k:n-A2 **exult**

Hknw: exultation

Hknw H-k:n-nw*N33:Z2 **oil**

HtA H-t:U30-A-P5 **a sail**

HtAw H-t:U30-A-w-P5 **a sail**

HtAw H-t:U30-A-w-S28:Z2 **awning**

Htyt H-t-i-i-t-F10 **throat, wind-pipe**

 **Htp** Htp:t*p **to be satisfied, be at peace, go to rest, set (of sun), to satisfy, make content**

 **Htp** Htp:t*p **peace, contentment, safe, offering** (which satisfies)

 **Htp-di-nsw** sw-t:Htp-X8 **offering wich the king makes**

 **Htpwt** Htp:t*p-t-N18:Z2 **offerings**

 **Htm** H-st-G39-t **to equip**

 **Htm** H-t:tm-m-G37 **to perish**

 **Htm** H-t:tm-m-G38-G37 **perish**

 **Htm** H-st-t-G38-G37 **perish**

 **Htmt** H-Q1-t:M3 **chair**

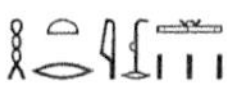 **Htr** H-t:r-i-M6-Y1:Z2 **team**

 **Htr** H-t:r-M6-Y1 **to tax, tax, assess**

 **Htr** H-t:r-E6 **pair of horses (team)**

 **Htri** H-t:r-E1 **team-ox (for ploughing)**

 **Hts** H-ti-s-Aa30 **celebrate (a festival), bring to and end, complete (period of time)**

 **Htt** H-t:t-O1 **mine**

 **Htt** H-t*t:N25 **mine**

 **Hdb** H-d-b-A15:D40 **throw down, be protrate**

 **Hdb** H-d-b-D54 **make a halt**

 **HD** T3-Z1 **mace**

 **HD** HD-S12:N33*N33*N33 **silver, lit.white gold**

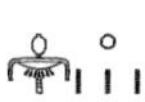 **HD** S14-N33:Z2 **silver**

 **HD** HD-D:N5 **to be bright, white**

 **HD-tA** HD-D:N5-tA:N23*Z1 **the day of dawns, lit. bright land, dawn, daybreak**

 **HD-Hr** HD-Hr **cheerful, lit. bright of face**

 **HDwt** HD-t-w-O18-O1 **chapel**

 **HDt** HD-t:E25 **white hippopotamus**

 **HDt** HD-t:S1 **the white crown** (of Upper Egypt)

 **HDt** HD-t-S28 **white clot**

 **HDi** T5-Z9:G37 **to destroy, injure, annihilate, put an end to**

 **HDi** HD-D:Z9-G37 **damage, destroy**

 **HDi** H-D:Z9 **damage, destroy**

 **Hdi-ib** T5-Z9:G37-F34:Z1 **to disobey the heart**

 **HDy** T5-i-i-Z9:G37 **annihilation, destruction**

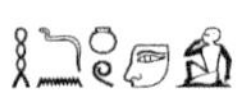 **HDn** H-D:n-nw:Z7-D19-A2 **be vexed**

x

	x	x	phonetic sound **x** (translates as the sound kh)
	xt	x:t	**thing**
	xt	x*t:Y1	**thing, property**
	iSt	i-S:t*Z9-Y1:Z2	**things, property**
	xt	x:t-Y1:Z2	**things**
	xt-nbt	x*t:nb:t	**anything, r-xt-nbt: more than anything**
	xt	x:t-Q7	**fire**
	xA	M12	**1000**
	xA	x-A-O1*Z1:.	**office** (administrative)**, diwan**
	xA	xA-A-O27	**office** (administrative)**, diwan**
	xA	xA-A-D40	**to examine** (a patient), **to measure** (grain)
	xAa	xA-A-a:D40	**to throw down, cast aside, abandon**
	xAa	xA-A-a-A24	**throw, put, leave, desert, throw down (ippopotamus)**
	xAi	xA-A-U9	**to measure** **xAw: measurer**
	xAi	xA-A-A24	**examine (a patient)**
	xAi	D40	**examine (a patient)**
	xAy	xA-A-V1	**measuring cord**
	xAyt	xA-A-i-i-t:Aa2-G37:Z2	**slaughter, massacre**
	xAw	xA-Z1:Z2	**lotus plants, plants**

Hieroglyphs	Transliteration	Signs	Meaning
	**xAwt**	x-xA-A-w-t-R1	**table of offerings**
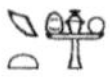	**xAt**	L6:t-R1	**table of offerings**
	**xAy(t)**	xA-A-i-i-R2	**table of offerings**
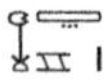	**xA-tA**	xA-tA:N23*Z1	**measure of area of 10 arouras**
	**xA**	M12	**measure of area of 10 arouras**
	**xAwy**	xA-A-Z7:y-N2	**night, late evening**
	**xAwy, xw**	x-w-O27	**night, late evening**
	**xAb**	xA-A-b-E25	**hippopotamus**
	**xA-s-bA**x	A-bA-s-N14*N14:N14	**the starry sky**
	**xAm**	x-xA-A-m-D41	**to bend the arm**
	**xArw**	xA-A-rw-Z1-T14-N25	**Khor, name of Palestine or part of it**
	**xArw**	xA-A-rw-Z1-T14-N25:Z2	**Khorians**
	**xArw**	xA-rw-w-A13	**Khorian**
	**xArt**	xA-A-r:t-G37	**widow**
	**xAs**	xA-A-z:D54	**scramble**
	**xAst**	N25:t*Z1	**country, foreign land, hill country**
	**xAst**	xA-s-t:N25	**hill country, forerign land**
	**xAstyw**	N25:t-tyw-T14-A1:Z2	**foreigners**
	**xAx**	xA-A-x:D54	**hasten, move quickly**
	**xai**	xa	**to rise (sun), to appear in glory (king)**
	**xai**	N28:a-Y1v	**shine, appear (of suns, gods, kings)**

xaw N28:Z2 **appearance**

xaw xa:a-Y1:Z2 **appearance in glory**

nb-xaw: nb-xa:Z2 **lord of crowns, epiphet of the king, lord of appearances**

xaw xa:a-w-N34:Z2 **weapons**

nw-r-a-xt: nw:Z1-r*Z1:a*Z1-M3:t*Z1 **of war**

xaw xa:a-Z7-xt:Z2 **weapons, funerary furniture, utensils, equipment, tackle (of ship)**

xaw-nw-aHA xa:a-Z7-xt:Z2-nw:Z1-aHA-A-A24

weapons of war

xr xa:a-r:D40 **rage**

xw x*x:x **exception, except**

xwi x:D43-w-Y1v **protect**

xw x:D43-w-S37 **a fan**

xw x*x:x **exclusion**

xww x:D43-w-w-G37:Z2 **evil**

xwfw <-x:f-w-> **Khufu, King Cheops**

Builder of the Great Pyramid at Giza. 4th Dynasty 2478 BC

nsw-bity-xwfw sw:t-bit:t-<-x-w-f-w-> **K.N.S. Khufu**

xwsi x:D43-w-s-A34 **pound, build, accomplish**

xwd x:D43-Z7:d-O38:Y1-A1 be **rich**

xb x-b-U7:D40 **detroy, overwhel**

xbA x-b-bA-a-mr:D40 **to ravage, destroy, subtract**

xbi	x-b-A32	**to dance**
xbi	x-b-Z9	**lessen, subtract**
xbyt	x-b-i-i-t-A14-Z3	**destruction, slaughter**
xbn	x-b-n:Z9	**be guilty**

xbnt: crime

xbnty: criminal

xbs	x-b-s-U7:D40	**cultivate, to hoe**
xbsw	x-b-s-Z9:Z2	**ploughlands**
xbsw	Z9:N21*Z2	**ploughlands**
xbswt	x-b-z-w-t:D3	**beard**
xbst	x-b-s:t-D3	**beard, tail**

xbstyw x-b-s-tyw-D3-T14-A40-Z3 **te bearded ones, ie. the inabitants of Pwenet (Land of Punt)**

xbd	x-b-d:G37	**disapprove of, blame**
xpi	x:p-D54	**walk, encounter**
xpt	x:p-A55	**deceased, death**
xpt	x:p-Z6	**deceased, death**
xpi	x:p-A14	**die**
xprr	L1-Z1	**dung-beetle, scarab**

xpr xpr:r **to become, be, to come into existence, exist, be, come into being, change (into), occur, happen, come to pass, take place, be effective, go by, be past, continue (of action)**

xpri	xpr-A40	**Khepri, the sun-god**

Transliteration	Code	Meaning
xprw	xpr-Y1:Z2	**evolution, development**
xprt	xpr-r:t-Y1:Z2	**things that happened, events**
xprw	xpr-w-Y1:Z2	**form, shape, manifestation, change**
xprS	xpr-r:S-S7	**the blue war crown**
xpS	x*p:S-F23	**foreleg (of ox)**
xpS	x:p-S:F23-A24	**strong arm**
xfa	x:f-a:D40	**seize, grip, grasp**
xfa	x:f-a:D49	**seize, grip, grasp**
xft	**x*t:f**	**when, according to, at the time of, when, (speech) to (someone), in front of, in proportion to, opposite**
xft	x*t:f	**when, according to, in front of**
xft-ntt	x*t:f-n:t*t	**in view of the fact that, since**
xft-r	x*t:f-Hr:Z1	**before the face of, in front of**
xfti, xftyw	x*t:f-A13	**enemy**
xm	x-m-D35	**to not know, to be ignorant**
xm	x-m-P5	**be dry**

xmw: dust

Transliteration	Code	Meaning
xm	x:R22-m-O49	**Ausim, Letopolis, a town L.E.**
xm	R22:O49	**Ausim, Letopolis, a town L.E.**
xm, xsm	x:z-m-O49	**Ausim, Letopolis, a town L.E.**
xm	x:R22-m-O20	**shrine**
xm, xsm	x:z-m-D35:O1	**shrine**

xmat x-m-a:t-M3 **handle (of oar)**

xmnw Z3A-Z3A-n:nw*w-O49 **El-Ashmunen, Hermopolis, a town in Upper Egypt**

xmntyw Z3A-Z3A-n:t-tyw-P1:Z2 **special kind of ships**

xmt x:D52-t-Z3A-A2 **think, foretell, expect**

m-xmt : m-x:D52:t-Z3-A2 **without, in (a person's) absence**

xmt x:D52-t:Z2 **three, do for a third time**

xmt-nw x:D52-Z2:nw **third**

xmt-rw D23 **three-quarters**

xn x:n-G41-A2 **phrase, utterance, speech, matter, affair**

xni x:n-G41-D54 **to land, alight, to stop, to rest**

xni x:n-i-D19:D40 **restrain**

xnyt x:n-i-i-t-G41-D54-B1-Z3 **dancing girls**

xnw x:n-G41-O1 **dwelling-place**

xnyt x:n-G41-D54-B1:Z2 **(strolling female) dancers, musicians**

xnw x:n-G41-Y1:Z2 **expense, expenditure**

xnp x:n:p-A24 **rob, despoil, offer**

xn-nfr x:n:Y1-F35 **a kind word**

xn-n-mdt x:n-G41-A2-n-md-d:t-A2 **proverb, saying, lit. word of speech**

xnm x:n-nm-m-D19 **smell, give pleasure to (someone)**

xnm x:n-nm-m-D19-A2 **breathe**

xnms	x:n-T34-m-s-A21-Y1:A1	**friend**
xnms	x:n-T34-m-s-A21-A1	**friend**
xnms	x:n-nm-m-s-A21-Y1	**to befriend, associate with**
xnmt	x:n-m-t-N33:Z2	**red jasper or carnelian**
mxnt	O48:n-t:N33A	**red jasper or carnelian**
xnr	x:n-r:U31-A24	**restrain**
xnri	x:n:r-i-U31:G37-A1	**prisoner**
xnrw	x:n-rw-F27	**reins**
xnrw	xA-n:Z2-rw:Z1-F27	**reins**
xns	x:n:z-D54	**fare through (marshes etc.), Khons, the moon-god at Karnak**
xnsw	x:n-sw-w-G7	**Khonsu** (the moon god of Karnak)
xnS	x:n-S:K5-G37	**to stink**
xnt	xnt-n:t-D19	**face**
xnt	xnt-n:t	**front, at the head of**
xnti: foremost of, he who is at the head of		
xnt	xnt-n:t:D19	**face, brow, front**
xnt	xnt-n:t:O1	**face, brow, front**
xnt	xnt-n:t-D19-O1	**harim, prison**
xnt	D19-t:O1	**harim, prison**
xnti	xnt-n:t-P1	**to sail upstream, travel south**
xnt	D19*t:N25	**Upstream (Nubia)**
xntyt	xnt-n:t-i-i-t:P1	**southward voyage**

xnty	xnt-n:t*y-I3-G7	**Khenty** (a crocodile god)
xnty	xnt-t:t*y-I3	**crocodile**
xntw	xnt-Z3	**racks for water-pots**
xntw	xnt-n:t*Z7-N23-Z1	**outside**
xntw	xnt-n:t-w-Y1	**before, beforehand, previously, earlier, previous, former**
xnt-S	xnt-t:S-N21:Z1	**wooded country, garden**
xntS	x:n-t:S-D19	**take pleasure**
xnd	x:n-d-D56-D54	**to trample, step on**
xr	x:r	**and, with, by, near (a god or king), under (a king's reign), (speak) to (a king), (come) to, before (a god or king)**
xr	x:r	**so says** (a person)
xr	x:r-A15	**Now..., Then..., Thus, Further**
xr	x:r-A15	**fall**
xrt	x-r:t-Y1:Z2	**state, condition, affair, requirement**
xrw	x:r-w-A15	**enemy**
xrw	xrw-Z7-D40:A1	**enemy**
xrw	A15	**enemy**
xrwy	x:r-xrw-w-i-i-A13	**enemy**
xrw	xrw-w-A2	**voice, sound**
xrw	xrw	**say**
xrw	xrw-Z7-X4:Z2	**invocation offerings**

Invocation offerings: the recitation of the offerinng formula:

All ancient Egyptian offering formulas share the same basic structure, but there is a great deal of variety in which deities and offerings are mentioned, and which epithets and titles are used. Below is an example of a typical offering formula:

sw-t:Htp-di-st-ir-nb-Dd-w-O49:t-Z1-nTr-aA:nb-Ab-b-N26:O49

Htp-di-nsw Wsir, nb Ddw, nTr aA, nb AbDw

offering-give-king Osiris, lord Busiris, god great, lord Abydos

'An offering whic the king gives to Osiris, lord of Busiris, thhe great god and lord of Abydos.'

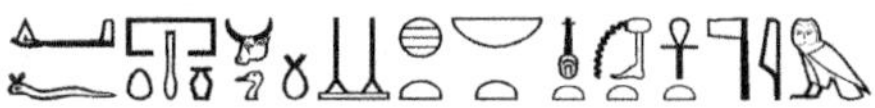

D37:f-O3-F1:H1-V6-S27-x:t-nb:t-nfr:t-wab:t-anx:t-nTr-i-m

rdi.f, prt-xrw-t-Hnqt, kAw Apdw Ss mnHt, xt nbt, nfrt wabt anxt, nTr im

to give.he, invocation-offerings-bread-beer, oxen fowl alabaster clothes, things all, good pure lives, god therein

'He gives a voice offering of bread, beer, cattle, birds, alabaster clothes and every good and pure thinng upon which a god lives.'

n:kA:n-i-Aw:x-i-i-wsr-s-r:t-z:n-A1-Aa11:xrw

n kA n, imAxy, sn-wsr-t, mA-xrw

for ka of, revered, Sen-wos-ret, True-Voice

'For the ka (soul) of the revered Senwosret, True of Voice.'

	**xry-fy**	P9-f:y	**so says, lit. voice-his**
	**xrp**	x:r:p	**to direct** (a project), **control** (affairs)
	**xrp**	x:r:p-S42	**director, leader, controller**

 **xrp** S42 **director, leader, controller**

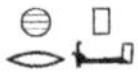 **xrp** x:r-p:D40 **manage**

 **xrp** x:r:p-S42-A24 **be at hand of, undertake, make offerings of**

 **xrpw** x:r-p*Z7:M3 **mallet**

 **xrS** x:r-S-M2 **bundle (of vegetables)**

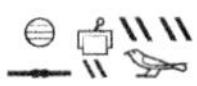 **xsAy** x:z-Aa18:y-Z4*Z4:G37 a **bribe**

 **xsy** x:z:y-M2 a **bribe**

 **xsbd** x-s-b-d:N33:Z2 **lapis lazuli**

 **xsbd** x-s-b-d:N33A **lapis lazuli**

 **xsf** x:z:f-U35-A24 **punishment, disapproval, to drive away, ward off, oppose, thwart, repress (crime), redress (wrong)**

 **xsf** x-s-U34 **spin**

 **xsfi** U35-P1 **travel upstream**

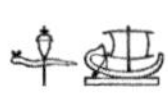 **xsfi** U35-P2 **travel upstream**

 **xsfw** xsf-f:D40 **opponent**

 **xsf-Hr** U35-A24-Hr:Z1 **defend**

 **xsf-r** U35-A24-r **contend against**

xsm: see **xm**

 **xsr** x:z:r-V29-A24 **dispel, drive away**

 **Xsr** X:z:r-A24 **dispel, drive away**

 **xx** x:x-F10 **throat**

 **xx** F10 **throat**

xx	x:x-F11	**throat**
xx	F11	**throat**
xt	x:t-Q7	**fire**
xt	x:t-Y1:Z2	**things**
xt	x:t-U30-A-N25	**Khatti, the land of the Hittites**
xt	xt:t*Z1	**tree, wood, lumber, stick, mast**
xt	xt:x*t-D54	**through, throughout, pervading**
xt	xt:x*t-D54	**wake, train, aftermath**
xti	xt:x*t-D54	**retire, retreat**
xtxt	M3:x*t-M3:x*t-D55	**retreat, be reversed**
xt	xt:x*t	**through, throughout, pervading**
xtyw	M3:x*t-tyw-O40	**terrace, terraced hill**
xtyw	O40	**terrace, terraced hill**
xtyw	M3:x*t-tyw-N23:Z1	**threshing floor**
xt-xt	M3:t-M3:t	**throughout**
xt-TAw, xt	M3:t*Z1-P5-M3	**mast**
m-xt	m-xt:x*t-D54	**after, following, accompanying, behind, afterwards, later**
xt-aA	xt:aA-G39	a type of **bird**
xt-xt	xt:x*t-xt:x*t	**to retreat, turn back**
xtxt	xt:x*t-D55-xt:x*t-D55	**reversal**
xtm	x:t-m-S20-Y1	**seal, to seal, to put under contract**

	**xtm**	x:t-m-O1	**fortress**
	**xtm**	tx:t-m-S20:Y1	**contract**
	**xd**	x:d-P1	**to sail north, to go north, to go downstream**

X

X

X X phonetic sound **X** as in German 'ich' translates as 'kh'

Xt X:t*Z1 **belly, womb, abdomen, body, innermost being**

Xt X:t*Z1*F51-A1 **generation**

XAt K4 **oxyrhyncus, a fish**

XAt XA:t-A55 **corpse**

XAt XA:t-A54 **corpse**

XAt XA:t*Aa2 **corpse**

XAt XA-A-t*Aa2:Z2 **corpse**

XAyt XA-A-i-i-t-Aa2:Z2 **heap** (of corpses)

XAr XA:r-V19 **sack** (dry measure of 20 **HqAt** 90.8 litres)

XAr V19 **sack** (dry measure of 20 **HqAt** 90.8 litres)

XArt XA-A-r:t-B1 **widow**

XAk XA-A-k:Aa2 **truncate, shorten, reduce**

XAk-ib XA-A-k:Aa2-ib:Z1-A14 **estranged, 'truncated of heart'**

XAt XA:t*O39 **quarry, mine**

XAt XA-A-t:N23 **swamp, marsland**

XAbt XA-b-t:V1 **bent appendage of the red crown** S3

XAbb XA-A-b-b-U2:U2 **crookedness**

xAbb xA-A-b-b-U2:U2 **crookedness**

XAmi	XA-A-m-D32	**bow down, bend (arms, back)**
XAr	XA-A-r:V19	**sack, a large measure of capacity**
XArt	XA-A-r:t-D3-B1	**widow**
xArt	xA-A-r:t-D3-B1	**widow**
XAXAti	XA-A-XA-A-ti-N4	**tempest**
XAk-ib	XA-A-k-ib:Z1-A13	**disaffected, rebellious, rebel**
Xam	X:a-m-D54	**approach (with hostile intent)**
xam	xa:a-m-D54	**approach (with hostile intent)**
Xaq	X:a-q-U37	**to shave**

Xaqw: barber

XpA	X:p-G41-A-Aa2	**navel, navel-string**
Xpw	X:p-w-Aa2:Z2	**sculptured reliefs**
Xpw	Aa2:Z2	**sculptured reliefs**
Xpn	X:p:n-F2	**fat (to be fat)**
Xms	X-m-s-D41	**bend (the back)**
Xn	Xn:n-S28	**tent**
Xn	Xn:n-D54	**approach**
Xni	D33:n-P1	**to row, transport by boat**

mXnt: G20-Xn:n-t:P1 **ferry-boat**

mXnty: ferry-man

Xnty: D33:n-t-A22 **statue**

Xnt	D33:n-t:P1	**excursion (in a rowboat)**

X

Xnt	Xn:n-t-F27	**hide, skin**
Xnyt	D33:n-i-i-t-A1:Z2	**crew**
Xnw	Xn:n-nw-w-O1	**interior, home, capital**
Xnw	Xn:n-nw-Z7-O49:O1	**royal court**
m-Xnw	m-Xn:n-nw-w-O1	**within, on the inside of**
Xnw	Xn:n-Aa2:Y1	**within, on the inside of**
Xni	D33:n-P1-A24	**to row** (a boat)
Xnw	Xn-nw-w-n:n:n-N36	**brook**
Xnm	Xnm-m	**join, unite**
Xnmw	Xnm-w-A40	**Khenum (god)**
Xnmw	Xnm-Z7-A1*B1:Z2	**house-mates, associates**
Xnwm	W9-E10	**Khenum**

Khenum: the ram god of creation and the waters, god of the First Cataract

Xnwm	Xnm-w-C4	**Khenum**
Xnwm-Htp	W9-E10-Htp:t*p	**Khenum-hotep** (man's name)
Xnnmt	Xnm-m-t-N35A	**well (in the desert)**
Xnmt	Xnm-t:N41	**well (in the desert)**
Xnn	D33-n:n-E20	**destroy, disturb**
Xnnw	D33-n:n-E20-D40:Z2	**turmoil**
Xnty	D33-n:t-A22	**statue, picture**
Xnty	Xn:n-t:y-A53	**statue, picture**

X

Xr Xr:r **under, under a burden, bearing, carrying, holding, having, being in (a state or condition)**

Xri Xr:r **lower, underlying, having**

Xrt Xr:r-t:Y1:Z2 **belongings, property, possessions, obligation, requirement, demnd, duty**

Xrt-hrw-nt-ra-nnb Xr:r:t-N5:Z1-n:t-N5*Z1:V30

under-day-of-sun-every: in the course of every day, lit. under every day of the sun

Xrt-Hrw N7 **daytime, course of day, under the day/sun**

Xrt-nTr nTr-Xr:r-N25 **necropolis**

Xrt-nTr R10-t:N25 **necropolis**

Xrt-nTr R10 **necropolis**

Xry Xr:r-y **who/which is under, (onne) who is suffering from** (a medical condition), **having, possession**

Xry-Hbt Xr:r-H-b-W3:N5-A1 **lector priest**

Xry-qni Xr:r-q:n-i-V19-A1 **porter, lit. one under the baggage**

Xrw Xr:r-w-N23 **underside**

r-Xrw r-Xr:r-w-N23 **below, dowwards**

Xrd X:r-d-A17-A1 **boy, child**

Xrd A17 **boy, child**

Xrdw X:r-d-A17-Z3 **childhood**

Xs X:z-G37 **vile, cowardly, weak, of humble status, of modest means**

Xsy X:z-y:G37 **wretched, miserable, vile**

 **XsAyt** X:z-A-i-i-t-N33:Z2 type of **spice**

 **Xkr** X:k:r-Aa30-Y1v **be adorned**

 **Xkrw** Aa30-w-Y1:N33A **ornament**

 **Xkryt-nsw** sw-t:Aa30 **king's ornament, title of a royal concubine**

 **Xkrw** Aa30-w-Y1:N33A **collection** (of war accoutrements)

 **Xdb** X:d-b-A24 **kill**

 s

	s	s	phonetic sound **s**
	s(z)	z	phonetic sound **s** (originally **z**)
	**s**	z:A1*Z1	**man**
	**s**	z:A50	**man**
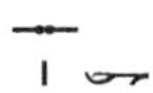	**s**	z:Z1-M3	**(door) bolt**
	**sn-wsrt**	wsr-s-r:t:z:n	**Senwosret** (man's name)
	**sn-wsrt-snbw**	wsr-s-r:t:z:n-s-n:b	**Senwosret-Sonbu** (man's name)
	**st**	z:t-B1	**woman**
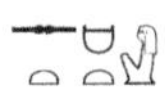	**st-Hmt**	z:t-N42:t-B1	**woman**
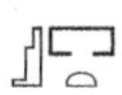	**st**	st-O1:t	**place, seat, throne, space, proper place**
	**m-st-iry**	m-st-O1:t-i-r:y	**in good order, lit. in their proper places**
	**st-ib**	st-F34-Z1	**affection**
	**st-a**	st-t:a*Z1-G7:Z2	**strike, blow** (of god's against people)
	**st**	z:t-G39	**pintail duck**
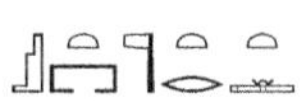	**st-nTryt**	st-t:O1-nTr-t:r-t:Y1	**divine state**
	**st-Hr**	st-t:O1-D2	**care, charge, supervision**
	**st-wab**	st-t:O1-s-wab-n:n:n	**purity, cleanliness**
	**st-skA**	st-t:O1-s-kA-a-U13:a	**ploughing**
	**st-StA**	st-t:O1-S:t*U30-A-Y1:Z2	**mysteries**

	sA	Aa18-Z1	**back**
	sA	Aa18-Z1:O1	**cattle-pen, outside**
	sAt	s-Aa18-A-t-O36	**outer wall**
	m-sA	m-Aa18:Z1	**after, in the back of**
	sA	G39-Z1-A1	**son**
	sA	sA-Z1	**back**
	sA	V16	**protection (magical)**
	sA	V17-Z1	**protection (magical)**
	sAi	s-sA-A-A2	**become sated, be wise, understanding**
	sAi	z:G39-A-A47-D54	**linger, lag**
	sAw	V17-w-A1	**magician**
	sAw	z:G39-A-w-A47	**guard, protect**
	sAw	A47-A-w-A24	**guard, protect**
	sAw	z:G39-A-w-M3	**beam, plank**
	sAw	z:G39-A-w-O49	**Sa el-Hagar, Sais, a town in Lower Egypt**
	sAwi	s-Aw-w	**extend, lengthen**
	sAwy	D22	**two-thirds**
	sAwt	z:G39-w-t:O49	**Asyut, Lycopolis, a town in Upper Egypt**
	sAb-Swt	s-Ab-b-Sw-t:Z1-H5	**variegated of feathers, an epiphet of the solar Horus**
	sAb	E17	**jackal, dignitary, worthy**

sAmt	Aa18-Z1-m:t-D3	**mourning**
sA-nsw	sw-t:n-G39-A1	**prince, lit. king's son**
sA-nsw	sw-G39	**king's son**
sA-nht	G39-n:h-t-M1:M3-A1	**Sinuhe** (man's name)
sAr	s-Aa18-A-r:T12-Y1v	**need, requirement**
sAirw	s-Aa18-A-i-r:T12-G37:Z2	**need**
sArt	s-Aa18-A-r:t-T12-A2	**wisdom, understanding**
sA-si	G39-A1-z:A1*Z1	**gentry 'son of a man'**
sAt	G39-t:.-B1	**daughter**
sAt-spdw	M44-w-G39-t:.	**Sat-Sopdu** (woman's name)
sA	V17-A1:Z2	**phyle** (class of priests)**, regiment, company** (of troops)
sA, sAw	V17-Z1	**protection, safeguard**
sA	V16:Y1	**protection, safeguard**
sAsA	s-sA-s-sA-A-D54	**attack headlong, push back**
sAw	V17-Z1-Y1:Z2	**protection** (by charm or spells)
sAi	A47-A-A24	**to guard, watch, ward off**
sAA-ti	A47-A-A-A24-ti-i	**beware, take care not to do**
sAH	s-sA-A-H-D61-Z1:F51	**toe**
sAH	s-Aa18-A-H-D61-D54	**to arrive at, to reach, to endow**
sAH	s-Aa18-A-H-D61:Y1	**to arrive at, to reach, to endow**
sAH	s-sA-A-H-D61-N21:Z1	**land given as reward**

Transliteration	Glyph codes	Meaning
sAH	s-sA-A-H-N14	**Orion**
sAH	s-Aa18-A-H-D61-N14-A40	**Orion**
sAHw	s-sA-A-H-D61-A1*B1:Z2	**neighbours**
s-Ax	s-Ax-x:Y	**make effective**1
sAXbw	Aa18-Z1-X:b-Z7-O49	**Sakhbu** (a place in the Delta region)
sAsA	s-sA-A-s-sA-A-D54	**overthrow**
sAq	s-Aa18-A-q-I5-Y1	**to pull (oneself) together, to be collected** (of mind), **collect, gater together**
sAtw	z:G39-A-t-w-N23:Z2	**floor, ground**
sAtw	G39-t-w-N21:Z2	**floor, ground**
sy	s-y	**her, it she**
sy	s	**her, it she**
sy	O35-y:D54	to **go**
sy	O35-G37	to **go**
i.sy	i-O35-y:D54	**go!**
sy	O35	**what? who?**
sy	O35-i-i	**how? why?**
sy-iSst	O35-i-V6:z-t-A2	**what?**
Hr-sy-iSst	Hr-Z1-O35-i-V6:z-t-A2	**why? for what reason?**
sy-nw	O35-n:U19-nw-Z7-N5	**when? at what time?**
siA	S32:Z1	**piece of clothe**
siAt	s-i-A-t:S32	**piece of clothe**

siA S32-A-A2 **to recognise, percieve, know**

siA S32-A-A2 **perception, knowledge, prognostication**

a type of medical text that shows how to predict the health of a patient

siA S32:Z1-A40 **Sia** (a god)

Sia - the god of perception

sip s-i-p:Y1 **to inspect, examine, to take stock, to inventory**

sipty s-i-p:t*y **inventory**

sin s-i-in:n-a **to smear**

sin s-i-in-Aa2:N23 **clay, plaster**

sinw s-i-in:n-Z7:D40 **to massage, rub**

sini s-i-in:n-D54 **to wait for, hesitate**

s-aAi s-aA:a-A-Y1 **make great, to increase (make bigger)**

sab z:a-b-Y1 **to equip (with weapons)**

sab s-a-b-T30 **castrate**

s-Ab z-Ab-Y1 **cause to tarry**

s-anx s-anx-n:x **make live, to nourish, to keep alive**

s-anxw s-anx-n:x-w-A1 **life-giver**

s-ar s-a:r:N31 **to cause to ascend**

saH E31-Z1-A50 **noble, privileged person**

sAH s-a-H-E31 **be noble, rank, dignity, nobleman, worthy**

sAH s-a-H-S20 **be noble, rank, dignity, nobleman, worthy**

sAH s-a-H-A53 **mummy**

	**saHw**	z:a-H-Z7-A51	**nobles**
	**s-aSA**	s-aSA:Z2	**to make numerous, many**
	**s-aq**	s-aq-q:D54	**introduce, to cause to enter, to send in**
	**s-iqr**	s-i-q:r:Y1	**make excellent, successful**
	**sw**	sw-w	**he, him, it**
	**swA**	s-wA-A-Z9	**cut off (limb), cut down (tree)**
	**swA**	Z9:T30	**cut off (limb), cut down (tree)**
	**s-wA, swAi**	s-wA-A-N31:D54	**to pass, escape from, pass away**
	**s-wAD**	s-M14-Y1	**to make green, to make flourish**
	**s-wAH**	s-wAH-H-Y1v	**set, make endure**
	**s-wab**	s-wab-n:n:n	**to purify**
	**sw**	N5:Z1	**day (of the month)**
	**sww**	s-s-s-w-N5:Z1	**dates (time)**
	**sww**	O35-w-N5:Z2	**dates (time)**
	**s-wr**	s-wr:r-A2	**to make drink, to drink**
	**swrd**	s-wr:r-d:G37	**to tire**
	**swn**	s-wn:n-T11:G37	**peris, suffer**

sswn: consume, destroy

	**swnw**	T11:nw*Z1-A1	**physician, doctor**
	**swn**	s-wn:n-T11:Y1	**barter**
	**swn**	T11:Y1	**barter**
	**swh**	s-w-h-A2	**boast**

swh	E20-A2	**boast**
swhA	s-Z7-h-A-A2	**to extol**
swHt	z:w-H-t:H8	**egg**
swsx	s-w-z:x*W10	**to widen, extend**
swt	s-w-t-P5	**breeze**
swt	s-w-t	**however, but**
swt	sw-Z7:t	**however, but**
swt	sw-t:Z1-M2	**a plant, sedge or scirpus-reed**
swt	sw-w-t:F44	**leg of beef, tibia**
swtwt	s-w-t-w-t:D54	**to go for a walk, to promenade**
nsw	sw-t:n	**king, (**He of the Sedge Plant)
sbi	O35-G37	**be faint, to perish**
sbi	O35-b-D54	**go, pass, send, load (ship)**
sbt	O35-b-D54-Y1:Z2	**load, transport**
sb-tw	O35:Y1-t-w	**in quest of, seeking for**
sbi-n-sDt	O35-G37-n-Z9:t-Q7	**burnt offering**
sbi-n-tA	O35-G37-n-tA:N23*Z1	**crumble to dust**
sy	O35	**what?**
sbi	O35-b-y:D54	**to send, to lead, accompany, to deliver, go, travel, attain**
sbi	s-b-i-Aa26-A24	**to rebel**
sbi	s-b-i-T14-A24	**to rebel**

Hieroglyphs	Transliteration	Code	Meaning
	**sbi**	s-b-i-T14-A13	**a rebel**
	**sbt**	O35-b-t-Y1:Z2	**load, cargo, burden**
	**sbA**	s-b-N14:Y1	**to teach**
	**sbA**	s-b-N14	**star**
	**sbA**	s-b-A-N14-N5	**star**
	**sbA**	s-b-N14-A-A24	**teach**
	**sbAt**	N14*t:Y1	**pupil (sbAty)**
	**sbA**	s-b-A-N14:O1	**door, gate**
	**sbA**	s-N14-b-O32	**door**
	**sbA**	O32	**door**
	**sbAyt**	s-b-sbA-A-i-i-t:Y1:Z2	**teaching, instruction**
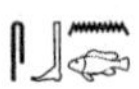	**sbn**	s-b-n:K5	**slip, go astray**
	**sbn**	s-b-n-D54	**slip, go astray**
	**sbnw**	s-b-n:D54	**go off course**
	**s-bhA**	s-b-h-A-D55	**cause to flee**
	**sbHw**	s-b-H-Z7-P5-Z5:Z2	**howling wind**
	**sbH**	s-b-H-F18-A2	**cry, cry aloud**
	**sbHwt**	s-b-H-Z7-t:F18-A2	**cries, wailing**
	**sbxt**	s-b-x:t-O14	**barrier**
	**sbxt**	O14-t	**portal**
	**sbx**	s-b-x-O13	**close (arms around someone), shut away from**

sbx s-b-x-O14 **close (arms around someone), shut away from**

sbx s-b-x-W24:Z1 **jar**

sbxt s-b-x:t-O21 **pylon shaped chest**

sbxt s-b-x:t-O32-O1 **gateway, portal**

sbxt s-b-x:t-O32-O14 **gateway, portal**

sbq s-b-q-D56 **leg**

sbq s-b-q-Y1v **be excellent, successful**

sbq D56-Y1v **be excellent, successful**

sbk, sbkw s-b-k:I3 **crocodile god, Sobek**

Sobek: the crocodile god

sbk-m-HAt I3-m-F4-t:Z1 **Sebek-em-hat** (man's name)

sbt s-b-t:F18-A2 **to laugh**

sbT z:b-T:D19 **to laugh**

sbty s-b-t:y-O36 **surrounding wall**

sp z:p*O50 **time, occasion, deed, act, misdeed, fault, matter, affair, venture, undertaking, success, accomplishment**

sp z:p*O50 **to happen**

spA z:p-pA-A-L5 **centipede**

spi z:p*O50 to **be left, remain, survive**

sp-sn O50:Z1*Z1 **twice, repetition:** indicates the reader sould repeat the word, phrase or complete verse

spAt s-p-pA-N24:t*Z1 **estate, farm, district, nome**

spAt	s-p*t:N24	**estate, farm, district, nome**
spAt	N24:t*Z1	**estate, farm, district, nome**
spAt	Aa8:t*Z1	**estate, farm, district, nome**
spAt	Aa8:t*O49	**estate, farm, district, nome**
spi	z:p*O50	**to remain over, survive**
spyt	z:p*O50-i-i-t:Z2	**remainder**
spr	F42:r-A2	**to petition, to appeal**
spr	F42:r-D54	**to arrive, approach**
spr	F42:r-A2	**petition**
sprw	F42:r-Z7-A2-A1	**petitioner**
spH	s-p-H-V1	**lasso**
spHt	s-p-H-t:F43	**ribs of beef**
spt	z:p*t-O50	**threshing floor**
spt	D24:t*Z1	**lip, edge (of pool etc.)**
spty	s-p:t*y-D24	**lips**
spty	D25	**lips**
spd	s-p:d-M44	**sharp, skilled**
spdw	M44-w-G13	**Soped (a god)**
spd-Hr	s-p:d-M44-Hr:Z1	**alert (person), astute**
spdd	s-p-d:d-M44	**to supply**
spdd	s-p-d:d-M44-Y1v	**to prepare**
spdt	M44-t:N14	**Sirius, Sothis, the dog-star goddess**

	sf	s-f:N5	**yesterday**
	sf	z:f-D19-A2	**be mild**
	sfn	s-f:n-D19-A2	**to be kind, merciful**
	sfn	s-f:n:nw*Z1	**to be kind, merciful**
	sfxx	s-f:x*x-V12	**to loosen**
	sft	z:f-t:T30-A24	**to slaughter** (animal)
	sft	z:f-t:T30	**sword**
	sft	s-f:t-W22:Z2	**oil (for anointing)**
	sfT	s-f:T-T30	**to cut up, butcher**
	sm	s-m-F37A:Y1	**to help, aid**
	sm	s-M21-m-M2	**herb, plant**
	sm	s-m-M21	**succour, tend, occupation, pastime**
	sm	s-m-M21-Y1	**succour, tend, occupation, pastime**
	smA	s-mA-A-T30:D40	**to kill, slay**
	smA	s-mA:T30	**to kill, slay**
	smA	S31-E2	**fighting bull**
	smA	Aa25	**a priest of Min, Horus etc, wose function was to clothe the god**
	smA	F36-Y1-A1	**associate, ally, accomplice**
	smA	z:mA-F36-F51	**lung**
	smA	F36-A-F51	**lung**
	smA	F36-A-Y1	**to join, unite**

smA	z:mA-F36	**be united, unite**
smA	F36-A-Y1v	**be united, unite**
smA	s-mA-D3	**locks, hair-covered part of head**
smAa	s-U4:a	**to make correct**
smA-tA	F36-A-Y1:tA	**to unite the land, to be buried, interment, juncture, fork (of road), burial, verge (of river)**
s-mAr	s-mA-A-r:T12-G37	**to impoverish**
smAyt	F36-A-A24-A1:Z2	**companion, confederates**
smi	s-mi-i-A2	**to report**
smi	s-mi-i-F27	a **lash**
smyt	z:t:N25	**desert, necropolis**
smyt	z:m-i-i-t:N25	**desert, necropolis**
smyt	Aa8:t:N25	**desert, necropolis**
smwn	s-m-wn:n-A2	**probably, certainly**
s-mn	s-mn:n-Y1	**to establish, to make firm, to perpetuate, to set up** (inscription)
s-mn	s-mn:n-U32-Y1	**to set, fix**
smn	s-mn:n-G38	**goose**
s-nmx	s-mn:n-x:U22-Y1	**to enhance, improve, to advance, to embellish, make functional, useful, to be of use**
smr	s-Ab-m:r-G37	**to inflict pain**
smr	s-Ab-A1	**courtier, friend (of the king)**

 **smr** s-Ab-m:r-A1 **courtier, friend (of the king)**

 **smr** s-Ab-m:r-A22-A1 **companion, Friend** (title: friend of the King), **smr-waty: Sole Companion**

 **smH, smHi** s-mH-H-n:n:n **flood, irrigate, cause to be in water**

 **smH** z:mH-H-P1 **skiff, light boat, small boat**

 **smx** s-m-x:D35 **to forget**

 **smx** s-m-x:D35-A2 **to forget**

 **smsi** s-ms-s-Z5 **to deliver** (a woman in childbirth)

 **smsy** s-ms-s-y:Z5 **to deliver** (a woman in childbirth)

 **smsw** A20-A1 **eldest, elder**

 **smsw** s-m-s-w-A19 **eldest, elder**

 **smsw** A19 **eldest, elder**

 **smsw** A20 **eldest, elder**

 **smdt** s-m-d:t-A1-Z3 **subordinates, staff**

 **sn** s-n:D19 **smell, kiss**

 **sn** s-n:Z2 **them, they, their**

 sn s:n **them, they, their**

 **sn** z:n:Z2 **them, they, their**

 **sny** s-n:y **dual, they two, them two**

 **sn** sn-n:A1 **brother**

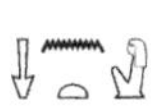 **snt** sn-n:t-B1 **sister**

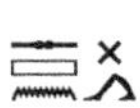 **sn** z:S:n-Z9:D54 **pull back**

Transliteration	Code	Meaning
sn	s-n-D19-A2	**to kiss, to smell, to breathe**
sn	sn-n:D19	**to kiss, to smell, to breathe**
sn	z:n:N37-O31	**to open**
sn	z:N37-O31:D40	**to open**
sni	z:n-X5:D54	**to pass by, surpass**
sni	z:n-N18:D54	**to pass by, surpass**
snw	z:n-nw-w-X4:Z2	**food offerings**
snw	s-sn-n:nw*D19-N18	**food offerings**
snwy	sn-n:nw-w-Z1*Z1	**two**
sny-mnt	z:n:y-X5:D54-mn:n-t-G37:Z2	**distress, calamity**
sn-nw, snw	sn-nw:Z1*Z1	**second** (ordinal number)
sn-nw	nw:Z1*Z1	**second** (ordinal number)
sn-nw	sn-n:nw-A1-Z1*Z1	**mate, fellow, companion, partner**
s-nwx	z:n-U19-nw*w-x-Q7	**boil, cook**
snb	s-n:b-Y1v	**healthy, safe, to be healthy**
snb	s-n:b	**recovery** (from illness)
snb	z:n-b-O36-D54	**overleap (wall)**
snb	z:n-b-W14	**jar of shape**
snb	s-n:b-Y1v	**be healthy**
snb-ib	s-n:b-ib:Z1	**famine**
snbt	s-n:b-t	**may you be healthy, Safe journey!**
snbt	z:n-b-O36	**wall**

 **snf** M4-M4-f:N5 **last year**

 **snf** z:n:f-D26-Z3 **blood**

 **snfA** z:n:f-P5-A24 **to vent**

 **snm** s-nm-m-A2 **to feed**

 **snm** z:n-T34-m-G28-Z8:N33A **food supply**

 **snm** z:n-T34-m-G41-G37 **sad, grief**

 **snm** z:n-T34-m-E20-N4 **torrential rain**

 **snn** z:n:n-V12 **document, deed**

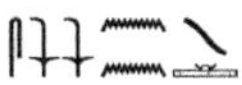 **snn** s-nn-n:n-Z5:Y1 **likeness**

 **snn** z-nn-A53 **image, portait**

 **s-nq** s-n:q:F18-A2 **to suckle, suck, nurse**

 **snt** sn-t:Z1 **flagstaff**

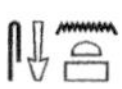 **snt** s-sn-n:t:O39 **base-block, base (of statue)**

 **snt** Z3A-Z3A-n:t-W3 **feast of the sixth day (of the month)**

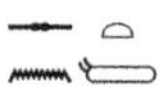 **snt** z:n-t:X5 **likeness**

 **snty** z:n:t*y-A53-Y1v **image, duplicate**

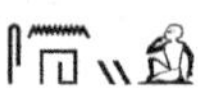 **snhy** s-n:h-y-A2 **muster (troops, workmen etc.)**

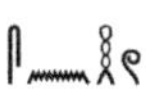 **snH** s-n-H-V1 **bind**

 **snHm** z:n-N41-m-L4 **locust, grasshopper**

 **snHm** z:n-N41-m-G38 **locust, grasshopper**

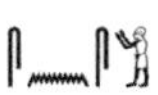 **sns** s-n-s-A30 **praise, adore**

snsw: adoration

	**s-xt**	z-n:xt:x*t-D40	**to strengthen**
	**snq**	z:n-q:D27	**suckle**
	**sntr/snTr**	sn-n:t:r-M6-N33:Z2	**incense**
	**sntr/snTr**	nTr-sn-n:t:r-M6-N33:Z2	**incense**
	**snt**	z:n:t-V5	**plan, plot out, found**
	**snT**	s-n:T-V5	**plan, plot out, found**
	**snT**	z:n:T-V5-N23	**ground-plan**
	**snD**	s-n:d-G54	**to fear, to respect, fear**
	**snD**	snD-A2	**to fear, to respect, fear**
	**s-nDm**	s-nDm-m-A17	**to make happy, to be seated**
	**s-nDm**	s-nDm-m-A7	**to sweeten, to reside**
	**sr**	z:r-G38	**a knid of goose**
	**sr**	z:r-E10	**seep, ram**
	**sr**	z:r-A21	**official, noble**
	**sr**	s-r-E27	**to predict, foretell**
	**sr**	s-r-E27-A2	**to predict**
	**sryt**	z:r-i-i-t-S35	**military standard**
	**srwi**	s-r-w-D40	**to remove**
	**s-rwi**	s-r-w-i-D54	**to remove**
	**srwx**	s-r:w-x:Z9-A24	**to treat (medically), to tend**
	**s-rwd**	s-r-w-d:T12-Y1	**to strengthen, to perpetuate** (offerings to the gods or ancestors), **to make flourish**

	**srf**	s-r:f-Q7	**warm, warmth, temperature, passion**
	**srf**	s-r:f-A7	**take rest, repose**
	**s-rmi**	s-r-m-D9	**to make cry, to cause weeping**
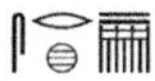	**srx**	s-r:x-O33	**banner, to contain orus name of king**
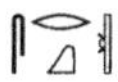	**srq**	s-r:q-Y1v	**relieve, admit breath to (wind-pipe)**
	**srqt**	s-r:q*t-L7-B1	**the scorpion goddess Serket**
	**srt**	s-r:t-M44	**thorn**
	**srd**	s-r:d	**glean, gather**
	**s-rd**	s-r:d-M31:Y1	**to plant, cause to grow**
	**shA**	s-h-A-E20	**disorder, lawlessness**
	**s-hAi**	s-h:A-D54	**to let down, lower, to bring down**
	**s-hri**	s-h:r-Y1v	**to pacify**
	**sH**	s-H-O22	**booth, arbour, council-chamber**
	**sH**	O22-Z1:O1	**booth, arbour, council-chamber**
	**sH**	s-H-O22-Y1v	**counsel**
	**sHwy**	s-H-w-y-G41-Y1v	**collect, assemble, assemblage**
	**s-Hri**	s-Hr-r:N1	**to distance, to distance oneself**
	**sHm**	s-N41-m-U32-a	**to pound, beat, pummel**
	**sH-nTr**	nTr-O21	**divine booth, shrine of Anubis**
	**sHr-nTr**	nTr-z:H-O21	**divine booth, shrine of Anubis**
	**s-HqA**	z-HqA-q-A42	**to install as ruler, to make (someone) a ruler**

s-Hqr s-H-q:r-G37 **to cause hunger, to let starve**

s-Htp s-Htp:t*p-Y1 **to satisfy, to please**

s-Htm s-H-tm-m-G39-G37 **to destroy, annihilate**

s-Htm s-H-st-m-G37 **to destroy, annihilate**

s-Htm s-H-t:tm-m-G41-G37 **to destroy, annihilate**

s-HD s-HD-N8 **to illuminate, to brigten**

s-HD s-HD-D:N5 **to illuminate, to brigten**

sH O22-Z1:O1 **tent**

sH O22-Y1v **advice**

sx z:x-A24 **beat**

sxw s-x-w-W10 **width**

sxt sxt-t:N23 **field, meadow, country**

sxt-iArw sxt-t:N21-i-A-r-w-M2:O49 **'Field of Reeds'**

A place in the Netherworld

sxt-mAt sxt-t:N23-H-mA-A-t-ti-N33:Z2-O49 **'Field of Salt' modern Wadi Natrun, NW of Cairo.**

sxty sxt-t:y-A1 **peasant**

sxA s-xA-A-A2 **to remember, to recall**

s-xa s-xa:a:Y1 **to cause to appear**

sxw, wsx s-x-w-W10 **width**

sxw s-x:W10-w-Y1 **width**

s-xwn s-x-wn:n-A2 **to dispute, dispute**

s-xpr s-xpr **to create, to bring into existence, cause to be, bring about**

s-xpr s-xpr-r **to bring about, make become, create**

sxr z:x:r-T11-A24 **to sweep, to overlay** (apply gold leaf)

s-xr s-x:r-A15-A24 **to cause to fall, fell, overthrow**

sxr s-x:r-Y1v **method, plan, idea, advice, conduct, position**

sxry s-x:r-i-i-Y1-A1 **captain (of ship), manager, commander**

sxm sxm-m-D40 **powerful, to have power, to prevail, to control, power**

sxm S42-Z1 **a Power epithet of deities**

sxm s-x-m-S42 **sceptre of authority**

sxm s-x-m-M3 **sceptre of authority**

sxm s-sxm-x-m-D40 **to gain or have control**

s-sxm: strengthen

sxm-ib: violent

sxm sxm-m-A24 **have power, be powerful, power**

sxm s-sxm-x-m-A24 **have power, be powerful, power**

sxm-ir.f s-sxm-x-m-ir:f **potentiate, magnate**

sxm-ir.f Y8-m-A24-ir:f **potentiate, magnate**

sxmx-ib s-x-m-x-ib:Z1 **recreation, sport, lit. distraction of the heart**

sxmt sxm-m-t-I12 **Sekhemet (goddess of violence)**

sxmt sxm-x:t-C164B **Sekhemet (goddess of violence)**

sxmty sxm-x:t*y-S5 **the double crown of Upper and Lower Egypt**

sxmty sxm-x:t*y-S6 **the double crown of Upper and Lower Egypt**

s-xny s-x:n-y-G41 **to cause to land, to land**

sxnt z:x:n-t-O30 **post, support of heaven**

sxs s-x-s-D54 **to run**

sxs z:x:z-D54 **to run**

sxt s-x:t-A24 **to strike**

sxt s-x:t-T26 **trap, snare (birds), weave, make, form (Dbt bricks)**

sxt T27-x:t-D40 **trap, snare (birds), weave, make, form (Dbt bricks)**

sxd s-x:d-A29 be **upside down**

sx z:x-F21 **be deaf**

sX z:X:F21 **to be deaf to**

sXAk s-XA-A-k-S28-A24 **strain, empty to the last drop**

sXb s-X-b-A2 **swallow (food, drink)**

sXp s-X:p-A2 **swallow (food, drink)**

sXm z:X-m-A24 **exert oneself, act violently, cope with**

sXnn s-X:n:n-O37-D40 **demolish**

sxnn s-x:n:n-O37 **demolish**

sXr s-X:r-T11:a **to sweep, to overlay** (apply gold leaf)

ss z:z-Q7 **ashes**

ssAi	s-s-Aa18-A-A2	**to satisfy, to make wise**
ssy, rssy	s-s-y:N31	**quite, entirely, at all**
s-spd	s-s-M44-Y1	**to prepare, to make ready, to supply**
s-spd	s-s-p:d-M44-Y1	**to prepare**
ssmt, ssmwt	s-s-m-t-E6-Z3	**horses**
ssnDm	s-s-nDm-m-M1	**a species of tree**
sw, sww	s-s-s-w-N5:Z2	**dates**
ssH	s-s-H-T30	**smash, destroy**
sS	z:S-G48	**bird pool, nest**
sS	z:S-G49	**bird pool, nest**
sS	G49:N21*Z1	**bird pool, nest**
sn, (sS)	z:S-O31:D40	**to open**
sS	z:S-a	**pass, spread, spread out, strew, post** (sentries)
sS	z:S-D40	**pass, spread, spread out**
sS	z:S-D54	**pass, spread, spread out**
sS	z:S-Z9:D54	**spread out**
sS	z:S-Z9-O1	**threshold**
sS, zXA	Y3	**to write**
sS, zXA	Y3-Y1v	**to write, draw, paint, writing, book, letter**
sS	z:S-Y1:Z2	**writings, paintings**
sS, zXA	Y3-Y1v	**document, writing**
sS, zXAw	Y3-A1	**scribe**

Transliteration	Code	Meaning
sS-nsw	sw-Y3	**royal scribe**
zXA-qdwt	Y3-qd-w-t	**outline-scribe**
sSA	z:S-A-Y1	**to be wise, aware**
sSA	z:SA-A-F5:Y1	**prayer**
sSAy	s-SA-y-G41-A2	**pray, supplication**
sSAy	z:S:y-G48A	**nestling**
sSAy	s-SA-A-y-G41-A2	**pray, supplication**
sSAt	R20-t-B1	**Seshat, the goddess of writing**
sSAt	R21-t-B1	**Seshat, the goddess of writing**
sSw	z:S-Z9-w-S21	**ring or disc (of metal)**
sSp	O42:p-A24	**recieve, accept**
sSp	O42:p-N5	**daylight**
sSp	s-S:p-N8	**daylight**
sHn	z:S:n-Z9:D54	**pull back**
sSm	s-T30-m-D54	**to lead, guide, rule, govern, direct, show the way, conduct (work)**
sSm	s-T32-m-D54	**lead, guide, show, conduct**
sSm	s-T31-m-D54-Y1v	**guidance, scheme, state of affairs**
sSmw	s-T30-m-w-A1	**leader, guide, pilot**
sSmw	s-T30-m-w-D54	**director, leader, guide, ruler**
sSmw	s-T30-m-Y1:Z2	**situation, conduct, behaviour, procedure**
sSmw	s-T31-m-A40	**divine shape, form**

	**sSm**	T33	**butcher**
	**sSn**	z:S:n-M9	**lotus**
	**sSr**	V6:Z1-S28	**linen**
	**sSr**	V33:Z1-S28	**linen**
	**sSr-nsw**	sw-t:V33	**royal linen, fine cloth**
	**sSr-nsw**	sw-t:V6	**royal linen, fine cloth**
	**sSrw, Ssrw**	V6:r-w-V33:N33A	**bags**
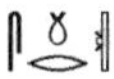	**sSr**	s-V6:r-Y1v	**thing, concern**
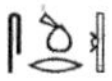	**sSr**	s-V33:r-Y1v	**thing, concern**
	**sSr, sS**	V6*Z1:Y1	**thing, concern**
	**sSr**	s-V6:r-A2	**recount, announce**
	**sSr**	V6:z:r-A2	**recount, announce**
	**sSr**	s-V6:r-U9	**corn**
	**sSr**	s-V33:r-U9	**corn**
	**sSr**	V6-Z1-U9:Z2	**corn**
	**sSr**	V35*V35:V35-U9	**corn**
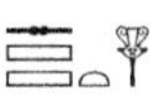	**sSSt**	z:S:S-t-Y8	**sistrum**
	**sSSt**	Y8	**sistrum**
	**sStA**	s-S:t*U30-A-Y1v	**secret**
	**sSd**	s-Sd:d-I3	**gleam, glitter (like a star)**
	**sSd**	s-Sd:d-V12	**head-band**
	**s-qA**	s-q-A28	**to exalt, extol**

Transliteration	Sign codes	Meaning
s-qbb	s-q-b-b-W15-n:n:n	**to make cool**
s-qbbwy	s-q-b-b-Z7:y-W15-n:n:n	**cool hall, bathhroom**
sqr	s-q:Aa7-T2	**to flatten, strike down**
sqr	s-q:r-Aa7	**smite**
sqr	s-q:r-T31:a	**smite**
sqr-anx	s-q:r-T30:D40-anx-n:x-T14-A1	**prisoner of war, living captive**
sqr-anx	s-Aa7-anx-A13-Z3	**captive**
sqdi	s-qd-d:N33-P1	**to sail, to sail on, to travel**
sqdw	s-qd-d-A30-A1	**sailor**
sqd	s-qd-d-A1	**voyager**
sk, isk	s-k	**lo, now,** enclitic particle
sk	s-sk-k	**to wipe out, pour one's heart out**
sk	s-sk-k:D40	**to wipe**
ski	s-sk-k-G37	**perish, destroy,**
ski	s-sk-k:D40	**to destroy, annihilate**
skw, skiw	s-sk-k:Z7-S154-A24-A1:Z2	**troops**
skA	s-kA-A-U13	**to plow**
skA	s-kA-A-U13-A24	**to plow**
skA	s-kA:U13-U7:D40	**to plow**
skA	s-kA-U13:N23	**to plow**
skm	s-km-m-D3	**grey-haired**
skn	z:k:n-I3	**be greedy, lust**

skr	z:k:r-G10	**the god Sokar of Memphis**
sgr	s-g:r-A2	**silence, stillness, quiet**
st	s-t	**them, it**
stA	s-t:U30-A-V2:D54	**drag, draw, flow**
s-tA	s-t:U30-A-Q7	**to light (a wick)**
stAt	V2:t*t-N37	**aroura, a field measure of about 2/3 of an acre**
stw	s-t:Z2	**they**
st	st-t:O1	**place, throne**
st, sT, sTy	s-t:Aa2	**fragrance, aroma, smell**
sty	s-t*y:Aa2	**smell, odor**
sty-r	s-t*y:Aa2-r:Z1-A2	**breakfast**
sti	s-F29-t-T11:D40	**to shoot**
sti	s-t-F29	**to shoot**
sti	F29-t:D40	**to shoot**
sty	F29-t-i-i-N35A	**pour (water)**
styw	s-t:F29-tyw-T14-A1:Z2	**Asiatics**
sti	F29-t:D4	**stare, stare at**
sti	F29-t:ir:T11	**stare, stare at**
sti	Aa32-t:N25	**Nubia**
styw	Aa32-t-tyw-T14-A1:Z2	**Nubians**
sty	Aa32-t:y-N33:Z2	**red, Nubian pigment**

styt	F29-t-i-i-t-D53:Z2	**procreation**
stwt	F29-t:t-Aa2:Z2	**shooting pains**
stwt	s-t-F29-w-t:N8	**rays of sun**
stp	stp:p-V6	**strip (of cloth)**
stp	s-t:p-U21	**cut up, choose**
stp	U21:p-Y1v	**cut up, choose**
stpw	s-t:p-w-stp:Y1-Z2	**the choicest, the pick**
stm	s-t-m-A1	**a priest who attended the toilet of a deity or deceased person**
stX	E20	**Sutekh (Seth)** a god **Seth - God of storms, desert, chaos and war**
stX	z:t:X-A40	**the god Seth**
swty, st	sw-w-t:y-C7	**the god Seth**
stt	F29-t:t-Aa2:Z2	**boil**
stt	s-F29-t:t-B1	**the goddess Satis worshipped at the First Cataract**
sttyw	s-t-F29-tyw-T14-A1:Z2	**Beduin**
stwt	F29-t-w-t-N5:Z2	**rays (of sun)**
stwt	s-t:F29-w-t:N8	**rays (of sun)**
stp-sA	U21:V16-O1	**palace**
stS	E21-A40	**Seth (god of disorder)**
sT, isT	s-T	**now**
sT, st	s-T	**them**

sTA s-V2:T-A-D54 **to drag, drag off (persons), to pull (wagon)**

stA s-V2:t-A-D54 **to drag, drag off (persons), to pull (wagon)**

sTAt V2:t*t-O39 **aroura** land measure of 100 cubits squared (2735 sq.metres, 2/3 acre)

stAw V2:t-w-Aa2:Z2 **secretions**

sty s-t:y-Aa2 **perfume, odour**

sty-r s-t:y-Aa2-r:Z1-A2 **time for breakfast**

sTA s-V2:T-A **drag, draw, flow**

sT s-T:Aa2 **fragrance, aroma, smell**

sTi s-T:D53 **engender, beget**

sTt s-T:t-F29 **engender, beget**

sTi s-t-F29-D53 **engender, beget**

sTi s-T:V33 **perfume, odour**

s-Ts s-T:z-U39 **to raise**

sTsy s-T:z:y-A98 **to be prostrate, sprawled out**

sTsy s-T:z:y-A29 **upside down**

sTsw s-T:z-U39-w:Z2 **support, supporting**

sTt sT-T:t-N25 **Asia, Sehel (an island in the First Cataract)**

sd s-d-S28-a **get dressed (in a kilt), to clothe**

sd s-d-F33 **tail**

sd z:d-Z9 **to break, to crush, to smash**

 **sdA** s-d-A-G33-Z1 **egret**

 **sdA** s-d-A-G33 **tremble**

sdAw: trembling

 **sdwx** s-d-w-x-Aa2:D40 **embalm**

 **sdb** s-d-b-A2 **to swallow**

 **sdb** s-d-b-S28 **fringe (of cloth)**

 **sdm** s-d-m-D7 **paint (eyes)**

 **sdm** s-sDm-m-D7 **paint (eyelids), eye paint**

 **sdgA** s-d:g-A-A30-D54 **to conceal**

 **s-DA** s-DA-A-D54 **go, pass by, pass away (die)**

 **s-DAy-Hr** s-DA-A-y:Z9-Hr:Z1 **divert oneself, amuse oneself**

 **sDAyt** s-DA-A-i-i-t:S20 **a seal**

 **sDAwt** s-DA-w-t-S20 **a seal**

 **sDAwty** S19 **treasurer**

 **sDAwty** S20 **treasurer**

 **sDAwt** S20:t-Y1:Z2 **precious things, treasures**

 **sDb** s-D-b-O30U **hindrance, obstacle, harm**

 **sDt** s-D:t-Q7 **fire, flame**

 **sDt** Z9:t-Q7 **fire, flame**

 **s-Dwy** s-Dw-y-w-G37 **to slander, vilify**

 **sDm** sDm-m **to hear, to listen, obey, understand, judge, satisfy (conditions)**

 **sDm-aS** sDm-A26 **servant**

	**sDmw**	s-sDm-w-A50	**judge**
	**sDr**	A55	**lie, spend all night**
	**sDr**	z:Dr:r-A55	**to lie down, go to bed, sleep, spend the night (doing)**
	**sDr**	s-Dr-A15	**to lie down, go to bed, sleep**
	**s-Dd**	s-D:d-A2	**to recount, relate, converse, talk, recite**
	**sDdwt**	s-D:d-w:t-A2-Z9:Y1	**quotations, literary works**
	**sDty**	s-D:t*y-A17	**foster child**

S

S S phonetic sound **S** as **sh** in 'shed'

S S:N23*Z1 **pool, lake, pond, garden**

Hry-S.f Hr-r:N1-S:N23:f-G7 Harsaphes (god, He who is on his lake)

SA SA:N23*Z1 **marsh, field**

imy-SA: marsh dweller

SA SA-A-E12 **boar, wild pig**

SA SA-A-Y1 **to ordain, to order**

SAi SA-A-i-E12 **pig**

SAw: pig

SAyt SA-A-i-i-t:Y1:Z2 **dues, taxes**

SAw SA-A-w-Y1 **fate, extent, bulk**

SAwAbty SA-wA-a-b-t:Z1*Z1-A53 **shawabti (Answerer: a small mummiform figure representing the deceased)**

n-SAw-n n-SA-A-Y1-n **to the extent of, in the capacity of**

SAa SA-A-a:Y1 **to begin, to (do something)**

SAa SA-A-a:Y1 **beginning**

SAas SA-A-a:z-X4 unknown **luxury product**

SAbw SA-A-b-w-X3*W22:N18-Z3 **food, meal**

SAmw SA-A-m-w-S28-Z2 **linen to be washed**

SAs SA-A-z:D54 **go off, proceed, to travel, go, make a trip**

SA-Htp SA-A-z:D54-Htp:t*p-O49 **Shutb, Hypselis, a town in Upper Egypt**

SAsw SA-sw-w-N25 **Shasu, the desert region adjoining Egypt to te East, the Shasu Desert**

SAt H7-t-N83 **Shaet, a country in the extreme south**

SAty SA-A-t*y:D40 **equivalent, equal**

SAd SA-A-d:D40 **to excavate, dig out, dredge**

Sd Sd:d-A24 **dig, dig out**

Sa S:a-N33:Z2 **sand**

Sa S:a-T31 **cut off (heads etc.)**

Say S:a-y-N33:Z2 **sand**

Sat S:a-t:F41-T31:Z2 **slaughter, ferocity**

Sat F41*t:Z2 **slaughter, ferocity**

Sat S:a-t-N33:Z2 type of **cake**

Sat S:a-t:V12 **dispatch, letter**

Saty S:a-t:y-S20-Y1:Z2 **measure of weight and value = 1/12 deben**

Saty S20-Z1:S **measure of weight and value = 1/12 deben**

Sad S:a-d:T30-A24 **cut off, cut up, cut down**

Sad S:a-d:F41-T30:D40 **cut off, cut up, cut down**

Sadw S:a:d-F41-T30:Z2 **incisions**

Sw Sw-Z7-N5 **sunlight, sun**

Swi Sw-w-N5 **be dry**

Sw Sw-w-A40 **Shu** (the god of the air)

Sw Sw-Z7:G37 **to be empty, devoid, lacking**

Swyt Sw-Z7-i-i-t:N5 **shadow, shade**

SwA S-wA-A-G37 **be poor**

SwA S-wA-A-G37-A1 **poor man**

s-Swa: impoverish, rob

SwAw S:wA-A-w-G37-A1:Z2 **commoners**

Sww Sw-w-w-M2:Z2 **a herb or gourd**

SwAb S-wA-b-M1 **persea-tree**

SwAbt(y) SA-A-wA-A-b-t:M3 **Funerary figure known as wSbty 'answerer'**

Swt H6-t:Z1 **feather**

Swt S36-t:Z1 **shade, shadow**

SwAw S-wA-A-Z7-A4-G37 **outcast, renegrade**

Sbi S-b-Z9-A2 **change, alter**

Sbt S-b-t-Z9-Y1:Z2 **exchange, price**

SbSb S-b-S-b-Z9:Y1 **regulate, transform**

Sbw S-b-w-N18:Z2 **food**

Sbb S-b-b-Z9-A24 **be mixed**

Sp S:p-D4 **be blind**

Sp S:p-D26 **to flow out, to pass out of**

Spsy A51-s-y:Y1 **noble, splendid, costly, elegant, luxurious (of gods), august**

Spsi A51-s-Y1v **be noble, rich**

Spsi S:p-s-A50 **be noble, rich**

Spsw: nobleman

Spst: noble lady

Spss Sps-s-s-Y1 **fine, special, noble**

Spssw Sps-s-s-Y1:Z2 **precious things, luxuries, wealth, delicacies, riches**

Spst Sps-s-t-B1 **noblewoman**

Spt S:p*t-K7 **get angry, be discontented**

Sfi S:f-F7 **respect**

Sfw S:f-Aa2 **to swell**

Sft S:f-t-I12-B1 **Sheftu** (woman's name)

Sft S:f-t-F7 **ram's head**

Sfyt S:f-i-i-t-F7 **wort, dignity**

SfSfyt: dignity

Sfdw S:f:d-w-V12 **papyrus roll**

Sm Sm-m **to go, to walk**

Sm Sm-m-D54 **go, depart**

SmAw S-mA-A-m-w-A33-A1:Z2 **wanderers, strangers**

Smaw M26-a:w-N24 **Upper Egypt**

Smaw M27-O49 **Upper Egypt**

Smaw M26 **Upper Egypt**

Tp-Smaw: the southern end of Upper Egypt from Asyut or Thhebes to Elepantine

wr-mDw-Smaw: wr-M27-10:Z2 **a title for the greatest of te tens of Upper Egypt**

Sma-s	M26-z-S1	**the crown of Upper Egypt**
Sma	Sma-U9:Z2	**Upper Egyptian barley**
Sma	Sma-a:Z5-A2	**chant, to make music**
Sma	S-m-a-M26	**make music**
Sma	Sma-a-A2-A1	**singer, chanter**
Smayt	M26-i-i-t	**chantress, singer**
Smayt	M27	**chantress, singer**
Smaw	Sma-a-w-A2-A1	**musician**
Smaw	Sma	**Nile Valley**
Smw	S-n:n:n-N5	**summer (season)**
Smw	S:n:n:n-U9	**harvest**
Smw	S:n:n:n-U9:Z2	**harvest season**
Smm	S-m-m-Q7	**be hot**

xm: x-m-Q7 **hot**

s-Smm: to heat

Sms	Sms-s-D54	**to follow, accompany**
Sms-wDA	Sms-s-D54-w-DA-A-D54	**funeral procession**
Smsi	Sms-s-D54	**follow**
Smsi	S-s-Sms-D54	**follow**
Smsw	Sms-s-D54:Z2	**following**
Smsw	Sms-s-w-D54-A1	**follower**

Smsw Sms-w-A1 **follower, retainer, attendant**

Sn Sn:n-M1 **tree**

Sni Sn:n-V1 **surround, encircle**

Sni Sn:n-Z8 **surround, encircle**

Sni Sn:n-V1-A2 **exorcise, connjure, ask about**

Snt: encantment, spell

Sna Sn:n-a:D54 **refuse, bar**

Sna Sn:n-a:U13-A24 **repel, deter, turn back**

Sna Sn:n-a:E23-A24 **repel, deter, turn back**

Sna Sna:a-O1 **magazine, ergastulum (pit prison)**

Sna rw:a-O1 **magazine, ergastulum (pit prison)**

Sna Sn:n-a:U13-N4 **storm cloud**

Snaw Sn:n-a-w-U13:D54 **policing, control**

Snaw Sn-n:a-w-U13 **ban**

Sny Sn:n-y-D3 **hair**

Snw Sn:n-nw-w-D3 **hair**

Snwy Sn:n-nw:Z7-i-i-D3:Z2 **hair**

Snw Sn-n:Z7-A2 **to enquire into a matter, to investigate, to question (someone), to conjure, exorcise (an illness), to curse**

Snw Sn:n-nw-w-Z8 **circuit, cartouche**

Snw Sn:n-nw-w-V9 **circuit, cartouche**

Snw V10 **circuit, cartouche**

Snyt Sn:n-i-i-t-A21-A1:Z2 **courtiers**

Snyt	Sn:n-i-i-t-N4	**rain-storm**
Snw	Sn-n:Z8	**net, network, mesh**
Snw	Sn:n-nw-w-V1	**net, network, mesh**
Snw	Sn:n-nw-w-G37:Z2	**illness, disease**
Sn-wr	Sn:n-wr:r	**the Ocean supposed to surround the earth**
Snwt	Sn:n-nw:Z7-t:O51	**granary**
Snwt	O51	**granary**
Snwt	Sn:n-nw:t-A21-A1:Z2	**courtiers**
Snbt	Sn:n-b-t:G11	**breast**
Snbt	Sn:n-b-t:F51	**breast**
Sns	Sn:n-s-X2	**a kind of cake or loaf**
Snt	Sn:n-t:V1-A2	**to revile, curse, spell**
Snt	Sn:n-t:V1-A24	**resent, feel hostility towards**
Snty	Sn:n-t:y-G31	**heron**
SnT	Sn:n-T-A24	**to revile, denounce, oppose, punish**
Sndyt	Sn-n:d-i-i-t-S28	**kilt, apron**
Sndyt	Sn:n-d-i-i-t-S26	**kilt, apron**
Sndyt	S26:t	**kilt, apron**
SnDt	Sn:n-D:t-M1	**the Nile acacia tree**
Sndt	Sn:n-d:t-M1	**the Nile acacia tree**
Sri	S:r-i-A17	**little, lad, youth, young man**
Srr	S:r:r-G37	**to be little, small, diminished, lessened**

Sri	S:r-i-G37	**to be little, small, diminished, lessened**
Sri	S:r-i-O36-D40	**stop up, close**
Srt	S:r:t-D19	**nose, nostril**
Ss	S-s-O39	**alabaster**
Ss	V6:z-O39	**alabaster**
Ss	V6:W3	**vessels of alabaster**
Ss	V6	**vessels of alabaster**
Ssr	V6:Z1-S28	**linen**
Ssr	V6*Z1:Y1	**thing, concern**
Ssr	V6-Z1-U9:Z2	**corn**
Ssr	V6:z:r-A2	**recount, anounce**
Ss	V6:z-V1	**rope, cord**
SsAi	S-s-sA-A-F5:Y1	**plead, pray**
SsA	S:z-Aa18-A-F5:Y1	**to be wise, skilled, informed**
SsA	S-s-sA-A-E29-Y1	**wisdom**
sSA	z:S-A-Y1	**to be wise, skilled, informed**
SsA	S-s-sA-A-F5	**be skilled**
SsA	F5-Y1v	**be skilled**
SsA	F6-Y1v	**be skilled**
SsAw	F5-w-Y1:Z2	**treatment (medical), prescription, recipe**
SsAw	S-s-sA-A-w	**bubalis (a type of water buffalo), hartbeest (antelope)**

	Ssp	O42-p:D40	to take, accept, receive, take up (object)
	Ssp	O42:p-A24	receive, accept
	Ssp	O43:p-A24	receive, accept
 of 1/7 cubit	Ssp	O42-N11	palm, a measure of length
	Ssp	N11	measurement 'palm'
	Ssp	O42:p*N5	light, dawn
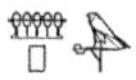	Ssp	O43:p-G7	image (of a god)
	Ssp	O42:p-A53	image, statue, sphinx
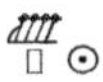	Ssp	O42:p-N5	white, bright
	Ssp	O42:p-N8	dawn, light, daylight
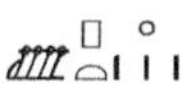	Sspt	O42-p:t-N33:Z2	cucumbers
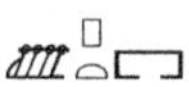	Sspt	O42-p:t-O1	summer house, room, chamber
	Ssmt	S:z-S15-m-t:N33A	malachite
	Ssmtt	S:z-m-t:t-S17A-B1	Shesemetet (goddess)
	Ssr	V6-s-r:T11	arrow
	Ssrw	V6	linen
	St	V1	one hundred
	StA	S:t*U30-A-Y1	mysterious, secret, difficult
	Styw	S:t-tyw-I2	turtle
	Stm	S:tm-m-A24	be insolent
	Stm	S:tm-m-A2	abuse (someone)

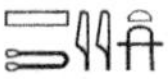	**Styt**	S:T-i-i-t:V19	**sanctuary of the god Sokar at Memphis**
	**Sd**	Sd:d-N21:Z1	**plot (of land)**
	**Sdi**	Sd:d-a	**to dig out, cut out, carve out, remove**
	**Sdi**	Sd:d-A24	**take, pull, rescue, draw forth, educate**
	**Sdi**	Sd:d-A2	**recite, read aloud**
	**Sdi**	Sd:d-D40	**recite, read**
	**Sdyt**	Sd:d-i-i-t:N23	dug out **pool**
	**Sdyt**	Sd:d-i-i-t:N23*Z1	**mound**
	**Sdw**	Sd:d-w-N23	**plot of ground**
	**Sdw**	Sd:d-w-F30	**water-skin, cushion**
	**Sdt**	Sd:d-t:O49	**Medinat el-Fayum, Crocodilopolis**

Sdty: te Shedetite, epithet of the crocodile god Sobek

q

q

	q	q	the phonetic sound **q**
	qA	q-A-A28	**tall, high, exalted, loud**
	qA	q-A-Y1	**tall, high, exalted, loud**
	qAA	q-A-A-N29:N23	**hill**
	qAa	q-A-a:D26	**spew out**
	qAa	q:a-D26	**spew out**
	qAw	q-A-w-N33:Z2	**grains**
	qA-sA	q-A-A28-Aa18-Z1	**arrogant, presumtuous**
	qA-xrw	q-A-A28-xrw-w-A2	**noisy, loud-voice**
	qAb	q-A-b-F46:Y1	**intestine, interior**
m-qAb		m-q-A-b-F46:Y1	**in the midst of**
	qAb	q-A-b-F46:F51	**intestine**
	qAb, qb	q-b-F46:Y1	**to double**
	qAH	q-A-H-N37	**earth, plaster**
	qAs	q-A-s-V1:D36	**bind, string (a bow)**
	qAqAw	q-A-q-A-Z7-P1	**travelling barge**
	qi	q-i-A53	**form, image**
	qis	A38	**Kis, Cusae, a town in Upper Egypt**
A39	**qis**	A39	**Kis, Cusae, a town in Upper Egypt**
	qis	q-i-s-O49	**Kis, Cusae, a town in Upper Egypt**

qsy A38-s-y:O49 **Kis, Cusae, a town in Upper Egypt**

qynA q*y:n-A-N25 **Qyna** (place name)

qaH q:a-H-D41 **elbow, arm shoulder**

qaH q:a-H-D41 **bend (arm, hand, people to one's will), turn one's back**

qaH q:a-H-D41:N21*Z1 **corner, bend (of stream), bight (of fishing net), fold**

qaH q:a-H-D41:N23*Z1 **angle, corner**

qaHt q:a-H-t-D41:N23*Z1 **district**

qbb q-b-b-W15 **(to be) cool, calm, secure**

sqbbwy: s-q-b-b-Z7:y-W15-N35A-O1 **bath-room**

qbb q-b-b-W15-n:n:n-Y1 **(to be) cool, calm**

qbH q-b-H-W15 **libate**

qbH q-b-H-W16 **libate**

qbHw: libation

qbH q-b-H-W16-N35A-N25 **Kebh, region of the First Cataract**

qbHw q-b-H-W16-N35A-G39-Z2 **birds of the marshes**

qbt q-b-t-W15-n:n:n **coolness, cool place**

qbw q-b-Z7-W15-n:n:n-P5-Z2 **cool breeze**

qfn q:f:n-Q7 **bake**

qfn q:f:n-N18 **cake, biscuit**

qmA q-T14-Y1v **throw**

qmA	q-mA-A-T14-G41-D40	**throw (throw-stick)**
qmA	q-mA-A-T14	**throw (throw-stick)**
qmA	q-mA-A-m-T14-G41-Y1v	**create, nature, form**
qmA	q-mA-A-T14	**to produce, create, engender**
qmA	T14	**to produce, create, engender**
qmyt	q-mi-i-i-t-G41-N33:Z2	**gum, resin**
qmyt	G41-i-i-t:N33:Z2	**gum, resin**
qmd	q-m-d-A2	**devise**
qn	q:n-A24	**to be brave, strong, sturdy, to conquer**
qn	q:n-Z9	**audacity**
qn	Aa8:n-Y1v	**be complete, complete**
qn	Aa8:n-V19	**mat**
qni	q:n-i-D32	**to embrace, embrace**
qni	q:n-i-V19	**sheaf**
qniw	q:n-i-w-D32-M3	**palanquin, carrying chair**
qnqn	q:n-Z9-A24	**beat**
qnyt	q:n-i-i-t:D40-A1:Z2	**braves**
qnt	q:n:t-A24	**valour**
qni	q:n-i-D32	**to embrace, embrace**
qniw	q:n-i-Z7-D32:M3	**palanquin**

Palanquin: an open seat on poles carried by porters

qnbt	q:n-b-t-O38-A1:Z2	**magistrates, (magistrates court)**

qnbt	O38-A1:Z2	**magistrates, (magistrates court)**
qnd	q:n:d-E32	**be furious, angry**
qri	q:r-i-E21-A24	**thunder, thunderstorm**
qri	q:r-i-E21	**cloud, storm**
qrr	q:r:r-I7	**frog**
qrs	q:r-s-Q6-D40	**to bury, burial**
qrs	q:r-s-A53-A24	**to bury**
qrs	q:r-s-M3	**burial**
qrs	q:r-s-T19-Q6	**bury, burial**

qrsw: coffin, sarcophagus

qrt	q:r-t:M3	**door bolt**
qrrt	q:r-r:t:O1	**cavern**
qrHt	q:r-H-t:W22	**vessel**
qrHt	q:r-H-t:W23	**vessel**
qrHt	q:r-H-t-I12	**local divinity, ancestral spirit**
qs	T19-Z1	**bone**
qs	q-s-T19	**bone, harpoon**
qs	q-s-T20	**bone, harpoon**
qsn	qs-n:G37	**pain, painful, troublesome, difficult, nasty**
qsn	q-s-qs-n:G37	**difficult, irksome**
qd	qd-d:N33:Y1	**to build, fashion**
qd	A35-A24	**to build, fashion**

	**qd**	qd-d:N33:Y1		**reputation, character, nature, extent**
	**mi qd.f**	mi-i-qd-d:N33:Y1-f		**in its entirety**
	**qdt**	qd-t:O39	**qidet**	a weight of 9.1 grams, 1/10 deben
	**qdS**	qd-d:S-N25	**Kadesh**	a city on the Orontes River
	**qdd**	qd-d:d-D4		**sleep**
	**qddw**	qd-d:d-w-D4:Z2		**sleep**

𓎡 k

	k	k	the ponetic sound **k**
	.k	k	**you, your, yours (masc.)**
	**kA**	k:A	**then..., next...**
	**kA**	k:A-A2	**then..., next...**
	**kA**	k-A-A2	**so** (a speaker) **will say**
	**kAt**	k-A-t	**device, thought**
	**kt**	k:t	**device, thought**
	**kAi**	k-A-A2	**think, plan, devise**
	**kA**	kA:Z1	**soul, spirit, mood, attribute, fortune, person(ality)**
	**kA**	D29	**soul, spirit, mood, attribute**
	**kA**	kA:D52-E1	**bull, ox**
	**kA**	E1	**bull, ox**
	**kA**	F1	**bull, ox**
	**kA-nxt**	E1:D40	**victorious bull, epithet of thhe king**
	**kAt**	kA:t-A9	**construction project, work**
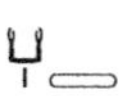	**kAw**	kA:Z1-N18	**food**
	**kAw**	kA:Z1-N18:Z2	**food**
	**kAw**	kA:D52-Z7-N33:Z2	**fruit, fruits**
	**kAw**	k-A-w-N33:Z2	**sycamore figs**

kAwt	kA:t-A9-Z3	**work, works**
kAp	R5:p-A24	**fumigate**
kAp	k:A-p:R6	**fumigate**
kAp	k-A-p:V19-O1	**hut, lean to**
kAp	R5:p-O1	**harim, nursery**
kAp	R5	**harim, nursery**
kAp	R5	**cover (in building)**
kAnw	kA:nw-M43	**garden**
kAny	kA:n-i-i-M43	**gardener**
kAny	M43-i-i	**gardener**
kAr	O18	**shrine, chapel**
kAri	kA:r-i-O18	**shrine, chapel**
kAri	kA:r-i-V19	**shrine, chapel**
kAry	kA:r-i-i-M43	**gardener**
kAhs	k-A-h-s-A2	**to be harsh, overbearing**
kAS	k-A-S:N25	**Kush** (in Nubia, place name)
ki	k-i-A2	**cry aloud, complain**
ky	k-i-i	**another, another man, another thing, another one**
kywy	k:y-w-y	**other, another**
ky	k-i-i-E32	**baboon, monkey**
.kwi	k-w-A1	**you, yours**

.kwi	k-w-i	**you, yours**
kfi	k:f-S28:D40	**strip, unravel**
kft	k:f-t:T30	**gash**
kt	k:t	**another**
kt-xy	k:t-x:y-A1*B1:Z2	**others**
kbi	k-b-i-A1	**Kebi** (a man's name)
kpny	kp:n:y-N25	**Byblos (Keben)** an Egyptian colony town in Lebanon
kpny	R5:p-n:y-N25	**Byblos (Keben)**
kf	k:f-S28	**to uncover, despoil (someone), plunder**
kfA	kfA-Y1	**to be discreet**
kfA	k:f-A-F22	**bottom (of vase etc.)**
kfA-ib	k:f-A-F22:Y1-ib:Z1	**trusty, careful**
kfA-ib	kfA-Y1-F34-Z1	**trustworthy**
kfA-ib-s(w)	kfA-Y1-F34-Z1-A1	**trusted man**
kfa	k:f:a-D49:D40	**to capture, capture**
kftiw	k:f-ti-w-N25	**Crete**
km	km-m	**black**
km	km-m-Y1	**to be complete, to come to a total of, to total up to**
m km n At	m-km:Y1-n-A-t:N5	**in the blink of an eye** lit. **in complete of moment**
km	km-m-D3	**black**

 **km-wr** km-m-wr:r-N25 the **Great-Black**

The Bitter Lakes in modern Suez Canal

 **kmt** km-m-t:O49 **the Black Land, Egypt**

 **kmt** km-t:O49 **Egypt, The Black Land**

 **kns** k:n-s-F51 **pubic region**

 **kns** F51 **pubic region**

 **ksi** k-s-A16 **bow down**

 **ksw** k:z-w-A16-Z2 **bowing** as in foreigners bowing to the king

 **ksm** k:z-m-D41:G37 **thwart, trat defiantly**

 **kS** k:S:N25 **Kush (northern Sudan)**

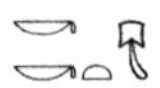 **kkt** k:k-t-F27 an unknown **animal** that eats grain

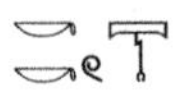 **kkw** k:k-Z7-N2 **darkness**

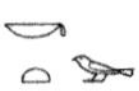 **kt** k:t-G37 **little**

 **ktt** k:t*t-G37 **small, trifling, little one**

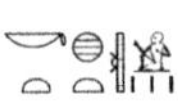 **kt-xt** k:t-x:t-Y1v-A1:Z2 **others**

g

g	g	the phonetic sound **g**
gAw	g-A-Aa2:G37	**lack, absence**
gAw	g-A-V32:G37	**lack, be narrow, sort of breath, deprive**
gAw	g-D19	**deprive of**
gAwt	g-A-w-t-V32:V32:V32	**bundles**
gwAwA	g-wA-A-i-i-Z8:Z5-D1	**throttle, choke, hold**
gwf	g-w-f-E33	**long tailed monkey**
gb	gb-b-A40	**Geb** (the earth god)
gbA	g-b-bA-A-D41:N23*Z1	**side (of room)**
gbA	g-b-bA-A-D41	**arm**
gb	gb-b-A40	**Geb (god of the earth)**
gbb	V33-b-b	**Geb (god of the earth)**
gbb	g-b-b-G38	**white-fronted goose**
gbtyw	V33-b-tyw-O49	**Kift, Coptus, a town in U.E.**
gbgbyt	g-b-g-b-i-t-i-A15	**fall headlong, fall**
gbgb	g-b-g-b-A15	**fall prostrate,**
gp	g:p-G37	**to cloud up**
gf	g:f-E33	**monkey**
gfn	g:f-n:D19	**to dismiss** (a person), **rebuff**

gm	gm-m	**to find**
gmA	g-mA-A-F51	**cheekbone**
gmw	gm-m-Z7-G37:Z2	**grief, mourning**
gmH	gm-m-H-D4	**to catch sight of, to spot, espy**
gmHt	g-m-H-t-S28	**wick**
gmgm	gm-m-gm-m-Z9	**to break, to crash, smash**
gmt	g-m-t	**black ibis**
gnwt	g:n-nw-w-t-T19-V12:N33A	**annals, records**
gnwt	T19-nw:t-V12:Z2	**annals, records**
gnwty	T19-T19	**sculptor**
gnwty	T19-t:y	**sculptor**
gnf, gfn	g:n:f-D19-A2	**to dismiss** (a person), **rebuff**
gnn	g:n:n-A7	**be soft, weak**
gr	g:r-A2	**be silent, silence**
grt	g:r:t	**however, moreover, now**
gr	g:r	**also, too, still**
gr	g:r-A2	**still, silent**
grH	g:r-H-N2	**night**
grH	N2	**night**
grg	g:r-grg	**snare, found, establish**
grg	g:r-U17:Y1	**to establish, re-establish, found, to prepare**
grg	g:r-grg-G37:Z2	**falsehood, lie**

	**grg**	g:r-grg-A2	**falsehood, lie**
	**grt**	g:r:t	**moreover**
	**grH**	g:r-H-N2	**night**
	**grH**	F27	**night**
	**grH**	g:r-H-D41:Y1	**end**
	**grg**	g:r-U17	**set up, found, establish**
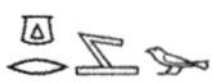	**grg**	g:r-U17-G37	**to lie**
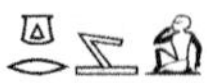	**grg**	g:r-U17-A2	**a lie**
	**grgw**	g:r-U17-G37:Z2	**lying**
	**gHs**	g-H-s-D56-F27	**gazelle**
	**gHs**	g-H-s-E29	**gazelle**
	**gHs**	D56-s-E29	**gazelle**
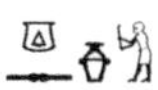	**gs**	g:z-W23-A24	**to anoint**
	**gs**	g:z-a	**anoint**
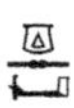	**gs**	g:z:D40	**get anointed, anoint**
	**gs**	gs:Z1	**side, half**
	**gsA**	g-s-sA-A-O37	**to tilt**
	**gs, gsi**	gs:z-D54	**to run**
	**gsw**	gs:Z1-w-A1*B1:Z2	**neighbours**
	**gsw**	g-s-w-gs-X7*X7:X7	**half-loaves**
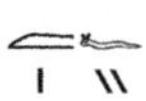	**gs-fy**	gs:Z1-f:y	**its two sides**
	**gs-pr**	gs:O1*Z1	**temple**

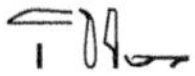	**gsti**	gs:Z1-ti-i-M3	**palette**
	**gsti**	g:Aa13-ti-i	**palette**
	**gs-tp**	gs:Z1-tp:Z1	**migraine headaches**
	**ggt**	g:g-t:F51	**kidney**
	**ggwy**	g-g-w-y-D5	**dazzled amazement**
	**ggwy**	V33-V33-w-t-D4:Z2	**dazzled amazement**

t

 t

	t	t	phonetic sound **t**
	**t**	t:X2	**bread**
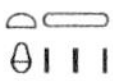	**t**	t:X2-N18:Z2	**bread**
	**t-HD**	t:X2-HD-M44	**white-bread**
	**tA**	t:A	**this, the**
	**tA**	tA:N23*Z1	**land, earth, ground**
	**tA**	tA:N21*Z1	**land, earth, ground**
	**tA**	t:U30	**kiln**
	**tA**	t:U30-A-Q7	**be hot**
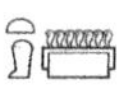	**tA**	t:U30-A-O16	**curtain**
	**tA**	t:U30-O17	**curtain**
	**tAyt**	t:U30-A-i-i-t-O16	**curtain**
	**tAyt**	t:U30-A-i-i-t-B1	**Tayet, the goddess of weaving**
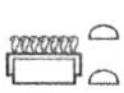	**tAty**	O16-t:t	**he of the curtain, epipet of the vizier**
	**tA-wr**	O17-G37	**larboard (port, port side, harbor)**
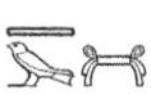	**tA-wr**	N17:wr-S22	**larboard (port, port side, harbor)**
	**tAy**	t:A-i-i-A1	**my (fem.)**
	**tAwy**	tA:tA	**The Two Lands, Egypt**
	**tAw**	N16:N16:N16	**lands, countries**

TA-wr R18 **This (nome of Abydos)**

nb-tAwy nb-tA:tA **Lord of the Two Lands**

Epiphet of the king, the Two Lands being Upper and Lower Egypt.

tA-mri tA:mr:r-i-M6-O49 **Egypt, lit. Land Beloved**

tA-nTr nTr-tA:N25 **God's Land**

tAS t:U30-A-S:Z9*N23 **boundary, border**

tA-smA tA:N23*Z1-s-mA-A-F36-N23 **landing stage**

tA-Dsr tA:Dsr-N25 **Sacred Land (necropolis)**

.ti ti **you, your (com.), hers (fem.)**

ti U33-i **you, your (com.), hers (fem.)**

ti U33 phonetic sound **ti,** enclitic particle: **yes, yeah**

ti U33-i phonetic sound **ti,** enclitic particle: **yes, yeah**

tiw U33-Z7-A2 **yes, yeah**

timHy ti-m-H-y-T14-A1 **Libyan**

tiHwy ti-H-w-y-N33:Z2 **peas**

tisw ti-sw-w-M3 **a stick**

ti-Sps ti-A50-s-N33:Z2 a type of **spice**

ti-Sps ti-Sps-s-M1 **a tree and a spice**

tit ti-t:Z1-O39 **pestle**

tit ti-t:Z1-V39 **the tyet amulet**

tit V39-t:Z1 **the tyet amulet**

tit t-i-t:D17 **figure, image**

	**titi**	t-i-t-i-A24	**crush, trample down**
	**titi**	t-i-t-i-D54	**crush, trample down**
	**.tywny**	tyw-n:y	**you, your, yours (plur. com.)**
	**.tywn(y)**	tyw-n	**you, your, yours (plur. com.)**
	**tw**	t-w	**one** (indefinite pronoun)**, this**
	**tw**	t-Z7	**one** (indefinite pronoun)**, this**
	**twy**	t-w-i-i	**one** (indefinite pronoun)**, this**
	**twA**	t-wA-A-A1	**inferior, a person of low status**
	**twA**	t-wA-A-A30-A1	**inferior, a person of low status**
	**twA**	t-wA-A-A30	**put a claim (on), claim from (someone), appeal to (someone)**
	**twA**	t-wA-A-A30-A1	**poor man, inferior**
	**twA**	t-wA-A-A19	**to support, support oneself**
	**tw.i**	t:Z7-A1	**I** (common singular)
	**twr**	t-wr:r-T19	**reed**
	**twr**	t-wr:r-A30	**show respect**
	**twri**	t-wr:r-i-T19-Y1v	**be pure, cleanse**
	**twnw**	t:Z7-n:Z2	**We** (common plural)
	**tw.k**	t*Z7:k	**You** (male singular)
	**twt**	t:Z7-t	**You**(female singular)
	**twtw**	t-w-t-w	**One**
	**twtnw**	t:Z7-t:n:Z2	**You** (common plural)

twy t-w-i-i **this**

twr, twi t-wr:r-i-qs-Y1 **show respect**

twt t-w-t:.-A53 **image, be like, statue, be fair, appropriate, be assembled**

twt t:t-A53-Y1 **to be in accord with, to resemble, be like**

twt ib Hna t:t-A53-Y1-ib*Z1-H-n:a **to agree with**

tbtb t-b-t-b-V1-D40 **hoist, to haul up**

tp tp:Z1 **head, on, chief, beginning, upon, (financial) principal**

tp tp:Z1 **upon**

tpi tp:p **who or which is upon**

tpi t:p-i-D19 **sniff, breathe in**

tpy tp:p*y **who or which is upon**

tpy T8 **who or which is upon**

tp-a tp:Z1-a:Z1 **before**

tp-m tp:Z1-m **before**

tp-Hry tp:Z1-Hr:r-A1 **master, cief, chieftan**

tp-dwAyt tp:Z1-sbA:t*N5 **dawn**

tpt tp*Z1-p:t-W23:Z2 **fine oil**

tpy tp:p*y **which is on, principal, chief, the best**

tpy tp:p*y **first**

tpy T8 **first**

tpyw-a tp:p-w-a:Z1-A51-Z3 **ancestors, those who were before**

tpyw-tA	tp:Z1-tA:N23*Z1-A1-Z3	**survivor, those who are on earth**
tpt	t-tp:p-W22	**first quality oil**
tpHt	t:p-H-t:O1	**cavern, hole (of snake)**
tf	t:f	**that**
tf, it	t:f-A1	**father**
tfA	t:f-A	**that**
tfn	t:f:n-G37-A1	**orphan**
tfnwt	t:f-nw:t-B1	**the goddess Tefnut**
itm, tm	t:tm-A40	**the sun god Atum**
tm	t:tm-m-Y1v	**be complete, perfect, be closed**
tmw	t:tm-m-A1*B1:Z2	**the totality (of mankind)**
tm	t:tm-m	(negative) (negates the sentence) **not do**
tm	tm-m	(negative) (negates the sentence)
tm	t:tm	(negative) (negates the sentence)
tm	t:tm-m-D35	(negative) (negates the sentence)
tmA	t:mA-A-V19	**mat**
tmA	t:mA-Aa6	**mat**
tmm	t:tm-m-m	**to close up** (wounds)**, shut**
tmt	t:tm-m-t:W22-D40	**to sprinkle, to dust (with a powder)**
tmt	ti-m-ti-m-A24	**sprinkle**
tmt	t:tm-m-t:M3	**sledge**
tmtm	ti-m-ti-m-A24	**to sprinkle, to dust (with a powder)**

Hieroglyphs	Transliteration	Code	Meaning
	**tn**	t:n	**this, that, you** (fem.sing.)
	**tni**	t:n-A19	**to grow old**
	**tni**	t:n-i-A19	**old age**
	**tni, Tni**	t:n-T14-G41-N31	**where?**
	**tni**	t:n-T14-G41-A2	**to distinguish**
	**tni**	t:n:y-T14-G41-Y1	**to distinguish**
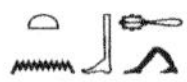	**tnbX**	t:n-b-X:D54	**shrink, recoil**
	**tnw**	t:n:Z2	**you** (com. plur.)
	**tnw, Tnw**	t:n:nw-w-T14-G41:Y1	**each, every**
	**tnm**	t:n-T34-m-D55	**go astray**
	**tnm**	t:n-T34-m-W22	**beer jug**
	**ti-nt**	ti-n:t	**she of**
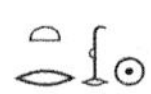	**tr**	t:r-M6-N5	**time, season**
	**tr**	M4-N5	**time, season**
	**tr**	t:r-M6-N5	**indeed, certainly, then**
	**tr**	t:r-M6-A2	**in truth, indeed, I suppose, pray**
	**tr**	t:r-M4-A30	**show respect for, awe of**
	**tr**	t:r-i-M6-A30-Y1v	**show respect for, awe of**
	**thi**	t:h-D56-D54	**violate, to go astray, lead astray, mislead**
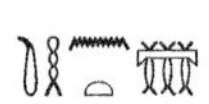	**tHnt**	ti-H-n:t-S17A	**faience, glass**
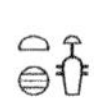	**tx**	t:x-U41	**plummet**
	**tx, txi**	t:x-W23	**to be drunk, get drunk**

txw: drunkard

	**txt**	t:x-t*W23:N25	**the land of darkness**
	**txb**	t:x-b-n:n:n	**to irrigate**
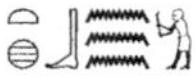	**txb**	t:x-b-N35A-A24	**immerse, soak**
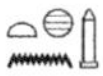	**txn**	t*x:n-O25	**obelisk**
	**txn**	O25	**obelisk**
	**txtx**	t:x-t:x-D54	**mess up, disorder**
	**tSi**	t:S-D56-D54	**be missing, go astray**
	**tSA**	t-SA-Z9:D40	**crush, smash**
	**tkA**	t:kA-Q7	**torch**
	**tkA**	t:kA-A-Q7	**wick, taper**
	**tkn**	t:k-n:D54	**be near, approach**
	**tks**	t:k-s-D54	**pierce, penetrate**
	**tkk**	t:k:k-A24	**attack, violate**
	**tti**	t:t-i-B1	**Teti** (woman's name)
	**tti**	<-t:t-i-A17->	**Teti** (woman's name)

 T

	**T**	T	phonetic sound **tj**
	**T**	T	**.T you, your, yours (sing. fem.)**
	**TA**	TA-Z1	**nestling, child**
	**TA**	TA-N33	**pellet**
	**TAi**	TA-A-D40	**take**
	**TAy**	TA-A-D51:D40	**take, gird on, rob**
	**TAwt**	TA-A-w:t-A24	**theft**
	**TAy**	TA-A-i-i-D53:A1	**male, man**
	**TAy**	TA-A-i-i-D53	**male, man**
	**TAw**	TA-A-w-D52-A1	**male, man**
	**TAw**	P5-w	**air, wind, breath**
	**TAw**	TA-w-P5	**air, wind, breath**
	**TAw**	P5	**air, wind, breath**
	**TAbt**	TA-A-b-t-U9:Z2	**loan of grain**
	**TAm**	TA-A-m-S28	**veil, lenience (veiling of the face)**

mTAm: clinging dress for girls

	**TAr**	TA-A-r:Aa19	**make fast, fasten**
	**TArt**	TA-A-r:t-Aa19:O1	**cabin**
	**TAs**	S24:z:Y1	**sentence (of speech)**
	**TAs**	S24:z-A2	**sentence (of speech)**

TAty TA-t:Z1-A1 **the vizier** highest official in Egypt

Tw T-w **you** (masc. sing.)

Twy T:w-i-i **this**

Tbwt S33-Z1 **sandal**

Tbt T-b-t-S33 **sandal**

Tb: be shod

Tbw: sandal maker

TbTb T-b-T-b-V1 **to hoist, to haul up**

TmA T-mA-V19-N21:Z1 **cadaster (property register)**

TmA T-mA-Aa6 **cadaster (property register)**

TmA V19-Z1:N23 **cadaster (property register)**

TmA-a T-mA-a:Z1 **strong of arm, strong-armed**

TmH T-m-H-T14-A1 **Libyans**

TmHw T-m-H-T14-A1*B1:Z2 **Libyans**

Tms T-m-s-Y3 **red**

tmsw ti-ms-z:w-Y3-G37:Z2 **hurt, injury**

Tn T:n **you** (fem. sing.)

Tnw T:n:Z2 **you** (comm. plur.)

Tni T:n-T14-G41 **where?**

Tni T:n-T14-G41-N31 **where?**

Tni T:n-T14-G41-A2 **to distignuish, to be distinguished, elevated**

TniA T:n-i-A-T14 **throwing stick**

 **Tny** T:n-y:O49 **This, town in U.E.**

 **Tnw** T:n-nw-w-T14-G41:Y1 **each, every**

 **Tnw** T:n-nw-Z7-T14-G41-A2 **distinction, eminence**

 **Tnw** T:n-nw-Z7-T14-G41-Y1:Z2 **number**

Note: the **T** in the above may be substituted with **t** giving: **tni** and **tnw**

 **Tnw** S15-n:nw*Z7-T14-N25 **Libyan desert**

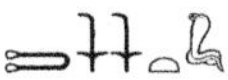 **Tnnt** T-nn-t-I12 **Tjenenet, goddess worshipped at Hermonthis**

 **TnTAt** T:n-TA-t-O40 **baldachin, raised platform for throne**

 **Tntt** T:n-t*t:Aa11 **baldachin, raised platform for throne**

 **Trp** T:r-p-G38 **a species of goose**

 **THn** T-H-n:D54 **draw near (to fight)**

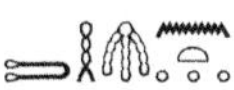 **THnt** T-H-S16-n:t:N33A **fayence, glass**

 **THnt** S15-n:t-N33:Z2 **fayence, glass**

 **tHnt** ti-H-n:t-S15-N33AV **fayence, glass**

 **THnw** T14-nw*nw*nw:N18 **Libya**

 **THnw** S15-n:nw*Z7-T14-A1*B1:Z2 **Libyans**

 **THH** T-H-F18-A2 **exult**

THw: exultation

THHwt: exultation

 **Ts** S24:Z1-V1 **vertebra**

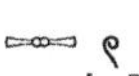 **Ts** S24:z-V1:D40 **to attach, join, knit together, to tie**

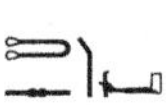 **Ts** T:z-T14-D40 **pick up, lift**

Ts	S24:z-V1:D40	**tie, bind, arrange**
Ts	T:z-S24	**tie, bind, arrange**
Ts	S24:z-A2	**saying, utterance**
Tst	S24:t*Z1	**troops, gang**
Tst	T-s-t-U39-Y1	**troops, gang**
Tst	S24:t*Z1	**knot, vertebra**

Tst: hill

Tsw	S24:z-w-A1	**commander, leader**
Tsi	T:z-Y1	**to raise up, lift up, get up**
Tsi	T:z-U39	**to raise, lift, to recruit, to rise, to mount**
Tsm	T:z-m-E14	**dog, hound**
Tt	T:t*Z1-R3P	**table (for food)**
Tt	R3P-t:Z1	**table (for food)**
Ttf	T:t:f-D54	**overflow, pour forth**
TTt	T:T-t:V1	**fetterer**

d

d

d	d	phonetic sound **d**
Drt, dt	d:t*Z1	**hand**
dA	d-A-G41-Aa2	**shake**
dAt, dwAt	N15-t:O1	**underworld**
dAt, dwAt	N14-t:O1	**underworld**
dAiw	d-A-i-Z7-N18:Z1*V6	**cloak**
dAiw	N18:Z1-S28	**loin-cloth**
dAiw	d-A-i-Z7-N18	**loin-cloth**
dAir	d-A-i-r:T12-A24	**subdue, suppress**
dAir	T12-A24	**subdue, suppress**
dAb	d-A-b-M43-N33:Z2	**figs**
dAr	d-A-i-r:T12-A24	**subdue**
dAr	T12-A24	**to control oneself)**
dAr-ib	T12-A24-ib:Z1	**to get control of oneself**
di, rdi	D37	**to give, offer**
di, rdi	X8	**to give, offer**
di-anx-Dd-wAs	di-anx-Dd-wAs	**given Life, Stabilityand Dominion**
dyt	d-i-i-t-M15	**papyrus plant**
diwt	Z2:Z4A-t-w-Z2:.	**set of five**
diwt	d:t:Z1*Z4B-A1-B1	**field labourers**

	**dyt**	Z2:Z4A-w-t-A2	**shriek, cry**
	**dyt**	Z2:Z4A-i-i-A2-Z1:Z2	**shriek, cry**
	**dwA**	sbA-A-A30-Y1	**worship**
	**dwA**	N14-A30	**adore (deity)**
	**dwA**	N14-A4	**adore (deity)**
	**dwA**	sbA-A-N5	**morning, tomorrow, rise early**
	**dwAw**	sbA-A-w-N5	**tomorrow, morning**
	**dwAw**	sbA-A-N5	**tomorrow, morning**
	**dwAyt**	N14-A-i-i-t:N5	**morning**
	**dwAt**	N14-A-t:N5	**morning**
	**dwA-nTr**	nTr-sbA-A-A30-A2	**to praise (thank)god**
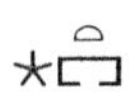	**dwAt**	sbA-t:O1	**Duat (the realm of thhe dead)**
	**dwn**	d-wn:n-D54	**to stretch, to stretch out**
	**dws**	d-w-s-A2	**malign someone**
	**db**	d-b-E25	**hippopotamus**
	**db**	d-b-F16	**horn (of animal), wing (of army)**
	**dbA, DbA**	d-b-bA-A-T25-Y1v	**replace**
	**dbi**	d-b-a	**to stop up, block**
	**dbyt**	d-b-i-i-t-F37-F37-W23:Z2	a type of **plant**
	**dbb**	d-b-b-D40	**stop up, block**
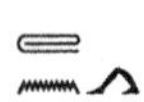	**dbn**	F46:n-D54	**to go around, circulate, travel around**
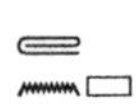	**dbn**	F46:n-O39	**deben** weight of 91 grams

dbn d-b-a-.-d-b-n:F46 **go around**

dbn F46:n-D54 **go around**

dbnw: circle, circuit

dbdb d-b-d-b-A2 **to pound** (heart)

iri-dbdb ir-d-b-d-b-A2 **to pound** (heart)

dbH d:F18-b-H-A2 **beg for, to request**

dbHw: a request, requirement

dbHt-Htp d:F18:t-Htp:t*p-N18:Z2 **the required offerings**

dp d:p-F20-A2 **to taste, to experience**

dp d:p-F20 **taste, experience**

dp d:p*O49 **Dep, part of Buto in the Delta**

dpt d:p*t-P1 **boat**

dpt-nTr nTr-P1 **god's ship, divine bark**

dpy d:p-i-i-I3 **crocodile**

dm d-m-T30 **be sharp**

dm d-m-T30-A2 **to pronounce, to mention**

dmt T30:t*Z1 **knife**

dmA d-mA-A-U32-Y1 **to stretch out**

dmA d-mA-M36:D40 **bind together**

dmA d-mA-M38:D40 **bind together**

dmi d-mi-i-N23 **town, harbour**

dmi d-mi-i-a **to touch, to reach** (a place)

 **dmi** d-mi-i-N23:Z1 **harbour, town**

 **dmd, dmD** S23-d:Y1 **total, unite, sum**

 **dmD, dmd** S23-d:Y1 **total**

 **dn** d:n-T30 **cut off (heads etc.)**

 **dni** d:n-i-V11-A24 **damm off, restrain**

 **dnit** d:n-i-t-V11-N23:Z1 **a dam**

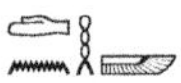 **dnH** d:n-H-H5 **wing**

 **dns** d:n-s-U32-Y1 **heavy, serious**

 **dns** d:n-s-U32-O39 **be heavy**

dns-ib: reticent

 **dr** d:r-A24 **to drive out, expell, remove**

 **dr** d:r:D40 **remove, repulse**

 **drp** d:r:p-A2-D38 **to offer, make offerings**

 **drp** d:r-p:D38 **offer food, feed (someone)**

 **drf** d:r:f-Y1 **title deed**

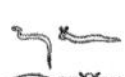 **Drf** D:r-f:Y1 **title deed**

 **drf** d:r:f-Aa10:Y1 **a writing**

 **dhn** d:h-n:D1 **to appoint**

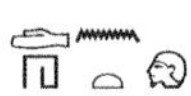 **dhnt** d:h-n:t-D1 **forehead**

 **dhn-tA** d:h-tA:N23 **to touch one's head to the ground**

(a gesture of respect)

 **dH** d-H-G37 **lowly, low**

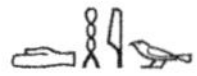	**dHi**	d-H-i-G37	**humiliate**
	**dHr**	d-Hr:r-G37	**be bitter**
	**dHr**	d-Hr:r-F27	**hide, leather**
	**ds**	d:z-W23	**jug, beer measure**
	**ds**	d:z-T30	**flint, flint knife**
	**dSr**	d:S:r-G27	**flamingo**
	**dSr**	d:S:r-G27	**red**
	**dSrt**	d:S:r-t-N25	**the Red land, the desert**
	**dSrt**	d:S:r-t-S3	**the red crown of L.E.**
	**dSrt**	d:S:r-t-W11	**red pot**
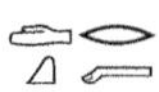	**dqr**	d:q-r:D51	**press, exclude**
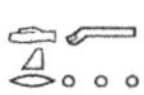	**dqrw**	d:q:r-D51:N33A	**flour, powder, fruit**
	**dgA**	d-g-A-D4	**to see, to look at**
	**dgi**	d:g-D5	**to look**
	**dgi**	d:g-A4	**to hide**
	**dgi**	d:g-A7	**to hide**
	**dgm**	d-gm-m-M1	**castor oil plant**
	**ddw**	D37:D37-w-O49	**Djedu, Busiris a Delta town**
	**ddwn**	d:d-wn:n-A40	**Dedwen, a Nubian god**

D

 **D**

Hieroglyphs	Transliteration	Code	Meaning
	**D**	D	phonetic sound **dj**
	**Dt**	D:t*Z1	**body, self**
	**Dt**	D:t*Z1-A1*B1:Z2	**estate**
	**Dt**	D:t:N18	**eternity, for ever**
	**DA**	A-A-Z9:M3	**fire drill** (stick for making fire)
	**DA**	DA-A-Z9:D40	**stretc forth**
	**DAi**	DA-A-P1	**to ferry (someone) across, to cross**
	**DAt**	DA-A-t:Z9	**wrongdoing, transgression**
	**DAyt**	DA-A-i-i-t-G37:Z2	**wrongdoing, transgression**
	**DAy-Hr**	DA-A-i-i-Z9:Y1-Hr:Z1	**divert oneself, amuse oneself**
	**DAis**	DA-A-i-s-A2	**contend, dispute**
	**DAisw**	DA-A-i-s-w-A2-A1	**disputant, adversary, opponent**
	**DAis**	DA-A-i-s-M2:Z2	**a type of plant**
	**DAmw**	DA-A-m-A17-A1	**young men, troops, generations**
	**DAmw**	DA-A-m-Z7-A17-A1:Z2	**recruits**
	**DArw**	DA-A-r-w-W8-A2	**need, requirement**
	**DArw**	DA-A-r-Y1:Z2	**need, requirement**
	**DArw**	DA-A-r-Aa2:Y1	**need, requirement**
	**DAy**	DA-h*y:N25	**Djahy, Phonecia**

D

DAt DA-t:D47 **hand**

DAtt DA-t*t:Aa8 **estate**

DAtt Aa8:t*O49 **estate**

DAtt N24:t*O49 **estate**

DADA DA-A-DA-A-D1:Z1 **head**

DADAw DA-A-DA-A-Z7-W24 **pot**

DADAt DA-A-DA-A-t:M3 **lyre**

DADAt DA-DA-nw*t:Aa8-A1:Z2 **magistrates, assessors**

DAdw DA-A-d-w-O27 **hall of audience**

DADAt DA-A-DA-A-t:M3 **harp**

spAt Aa8:t*O49 **district, nome**

Da D:a-T14-D54 **to spear, to harpoon (fish)**

Da D:a-P5 **wind storm, tempest**

Dabt D:a-b-t-N33:Z2 **charcoal**

Dam D:a-m-S40 the spiral **djam sceptre**

Dam S41 **the spiral djam sceptre**

Damw S40-m-w-S12:N33:Z2 **electrum** (mixture of gold and silver)

Dam S40-S12 **electrum**

Dam S14A **electrum**

Dar D:a-r:D54-T14 **to search, seek out, probe, investigate**

Dw	Dw:O39	**mountain**
Dw	N26:Z1	**mountain**
Dw	Dw-w-G37	**misfortune, evil, bad, wicked, sad**
Dw	Dw-w-i-A24	**evil**
Dwt	Dw-w-t-G37:Z2	**evil**
Dwi	N26-w-i-A26	**call (someone)**
Dws	N26-w-s-A2	**malign (someone)**
Dbt	G22-b-t:O39	**brick**
DbA	DbA-b-O36h:D40	**to block, stop up**
DbA	DbA-b-Y1	**to restore, repay, replace**
dbA	d-bA-A-DbA-Y1	**to restore, repay, replace**
DbAw	DbA-b-A-Z7-Y1:Z2	**payments, compensation, bribe**
dbAw	d-b-bA-A-Z7-DbA-Y1:Z2	**payments, compensation**
DbAw	T25-b-w-M3:Z2	**floats**
DbA	T25-b-Y1v	**clothe, adorn**
DbA	bA-A-T25-Y1v	**replace**
DbA	T25-b-O36h:D40	**stop up, block**
DbA	T25-b-O49	**Edfu, Apollonis polis, a town in Upper Egypt**
Dba	D50*Z1	**finger, finger breadth, as measure = 1/28 cubit**
Dba	D50	**10,000**

Transliteration	Signs	Meaning
DfAw	D:f-A-Z7-G41-Y1:Z2	**provisions, sustenance, abundance**
DfA	D:f-G42-N18:Z2	**provisions**
Df	D:f-N18:Z2	**provisions**
DfAw	D:f-G42:Z2	**food**
DfAw	D:f-D:f-D:f	**provisions, sustenance, abundance**
DfD	D:f-D:D12	**pupil of the eye**
Dnnt	D:n:n-t-D1	**skull**
Dnd	D:n-d-F2	**rage, to rage**
Drt	d:t*Z1	**hand**
Drt	Dr:r-t:D47	**hand**
st-Drt:	st-t:O1-d:t*Z1	**how to handle things, the way to act**
Dr	Dr	**since**
Dr	Dr:r	**since, to end up**
Dr	Dr:r-O36	**wall, enclosure**
Dri	Dr:r-i-D40	**be hard, firm**
Drit	Dr:r-i-t:M3	**wall, enclosure**
Dr-tyw	Dr:r-tyw-A51-Z3	**the ancestors**
DrDr	Dr:r-Dr:r-A30-A1	**stranger**
r-Dr-f	r-Dr:r-f	**limit, to its entirety**
Drw	Dr:r-w-N31	**limit, boundary, border**
Drw	Dr:r-w-F51	**side (of body, cariot etc.)**

D

Hieroglyphs	Transliteration	Code	Meaning
	**DrD**	F21:Z1	**leaf (of tree)**
	**DrD**	Dr:r-D-F21:Z1	**leaf (of tree)**
	**nn-Drw**	D35:n-Dr:r-w-N31:Z2	**witout limits**
	**DrDry**	Dr:r-Dr:r-i-i-A13*Z1	**strange, foreign**
	**DrDri**	Dr:r-Dr:r-i-A30	**foreign, foreigner**
	**DHwty**	G26:t*y-G7	**Thoth, Djhwty** (ibis headed god)
	**DHwty**	G26-A40	**Thoth, Djhwty**
	**DHwty**	D-H-w-t:y	**Thoth, Djhwty**
	**DHwty**	C3	**Thoth, Djhwty**
	**Dwty**	X2-C3	**Thoth, Djhwty**
	**Ds**	D:z	**-self** (as in Ds.f **himself**)
	**Dsr**	Dsr:r	**holy, sacred**
	**tA-Dsr**	tA:Dsr-N25	**the Sacred Land, the necropolis**

Dsrw: privacy

Hieroglyphs	Transliteration	Code	Meaning
	**Dsrt**	Dsr:r:t	**sacred area**
	**Dd**	D:d	**to say, speak, tell, talk**
	**DdA**	D:d-A-F5	**be fat**
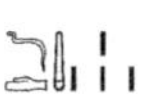	**Dd-mdw**	D:d-md-Z1:Z2	**words to be recited**
	**Dd-mdw**	D-md	**words to be recited**
	**Ddwt**	D:d-t:Z2	**sayings**
	**Dd**	R11-Z1	**Djed column**
	**Ddi**	Dd-d:Y1	**stable, steady, enduring**

Ddb D:d-b-T30 **sting, incite**

Ddft D:d-f:t-I14 **snake**

DdH D:d-H-V1:D40 **imprison**

Ddt Dd-d:t:Y1 **stability, duration**

Ddt Dd-d:t-O49 **Mendes, Tell er Ruba, a town in the Delta**

Ddi Dd-Dd-Y1:A1 **Djedi** (man's name)

Dd-snfrw, mAa-xrw Dd-Dd-Y1-<-s-nfr-f:r-Z7->-mA:Aa11-a-xrw-Z7-A2 **Djed-Sneferu, Justified (True of Voice)**

Ddw Dd-Dd-w-O49:Z1 **Busiris** (place name), Abusir Bana

Ddw D37:D37-w-O49 **Busiris** (place name), Abusir Bana

Ddw d:d-w-O49 **Busiris** (place name), Abusir Bana

Ddf D:d-f:Y1 **have goose-bumps (of skin), stand on end (of hair)**

Printed in Dunstable, United Kingdom

67199653R00157